The Road to Peace

Dedication

To:

From:

The Road to Peace

NATO and the international community in Bosnia

Rupert Wolfe Murray
Photographs by Steven Gordon

Foreword by General George A. Joulwan
Supreme Allied Commander, Europe

CONNECT

Endpapers:
Destroyed and booby trapped houses in the Serb held area around Doboj.

Half title:
A group of Bosnian Muslim children walking home at sunset, near Kalesija in northern Bosnia.

Frontispiece:
A US Army SFOR "Humvee" approaches an unlit tunnel on the road to Tuzla.

Opposite:
A group of Bosnian Croat HVO soldiers during a military training session with the private US company MPRI. Kiseljak, central Bosnia Herzegovina.

Acknowledgements

The Road to Peace was written as a snapshot of the huge international presence in Bosnia since Dayton and we apologise to any readers who expect this book to be a comprehensive study of NATO's Stabilization Force (SFOR) or the other international agencies represented in the book. The views expressed in this book are solely those of the author, and those interviewed, and do not necessarily reflect those of SFOR, NATO, UN, IPTF, OSCE, or ODA.

Apologies are due to all the people across Bosnia whom we interviewed but failed to include in this book, but what they had to say certainly contributed to my understanding of the situation.

We would like to thank all the people and organisations that helped us to put this book together, especially those who allowed us to interview them. In Bosnia thanks are due to everyone at AAFES and the CPIC offices as well as the following individuals: Guy Shields, Bill DuPont, Chris Bennett, Jasminko Arnautovic, Chris Steven, Ian McLeod, Angela and Milorad Vujovic, Annabelle Lund, the Sabanovic family, Drazen Marinic, Dino Cokic, Mirza and Nisveta Salkic and my long-suffering fiancée, Alina Boboc.

In Scotland the following people must also be thanked for their help: Janet Watson, Jim Hutcheson, everyone at Canongate, Paul Harris, Stewart Anderson, the trustees of Connect Humanitarian Agency and my brother Gavin. In Slovenia the printers Gorenjski Tisk are due a big thank you for their unflagging dedication to quality, and my thanks are due also to Igor Potocnik of Europapier.

The Road to Peace is dedicated to everyone who is committed to finding a peaceful solution in Bosnia Herzegovina. I also dedicate this book to Molly and Ian Gordon. Without their son Steven there would have been less laughter and no book.

Rupert Wolfe Murray
Edinburgh, UK, August 1997

First published in 1997 by Connect Trading Limited
17 Jeffrey Street, Edinburgh EH1 1DR, Scotland, UK
Telephone/fax: +44 131 558 9759
email: bosnia@dial.pipex.com

ISBN 1 901205 04 5

Text © copyright Rupert Wolfe Murray 1997
Photographs © copyright Steven Gordon 1997
Foreword © copyright George A. Joulwan 1997

Book design by Janet Watson
Cover design by James Hutcheson
Cartography by David Langworth

Colour separation by Gorenjski Tisk Printing & Publishing Company
Paper supplied by Europapier, Lubljana, Slovenia
Printed in the Republic of Slovenia by Gorenjski Tisk

Contents

The OTTOMAN EMPIRE before 1453

J.F.H.

From: History of the World, H. G. Wells (1933)

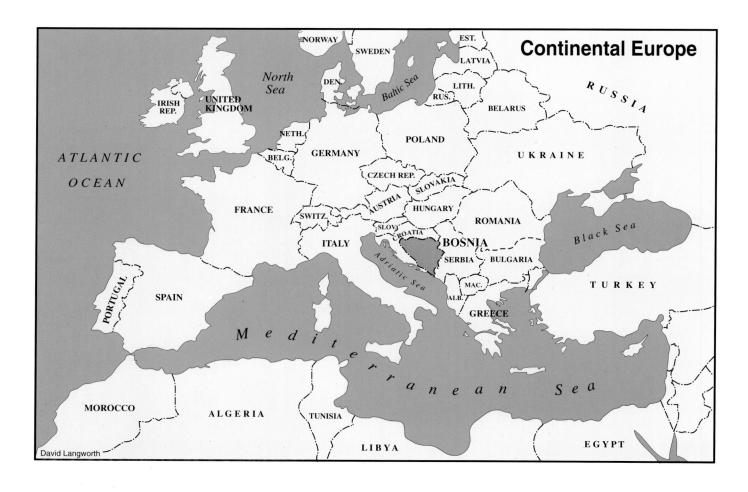

Continental Europe

David Langworth

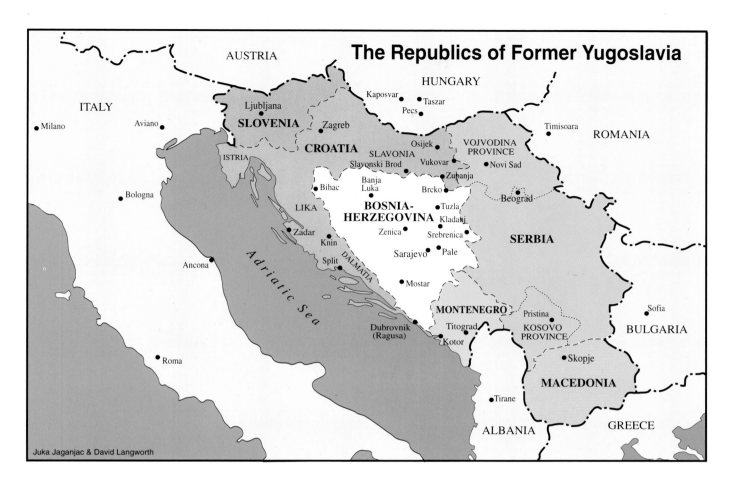

The Republics of Former Yugoslavia

AUSTRIA
HUNGARY
ITALY
Milano
Aviano
SLOVENIA
Ljubljana
Zagreb
CROATIA
ISTRIA
Bologna
LIKA
Zadar
Knin
DALMATIA
Ancona
Split
Kaposvar
Taszar
Pecs
Timisoara
ROMANIA
Osijek
VOJVODINA
PROVINCE
SLAVONIA
Slavonski Brod
Vukovar
Novi Sad
Zupanja
Banja
Luka
Brcko
Bihac
Beograd
BOSNIA-
HERZEGOVINA
Tuzla
Kladanj
Zenica
Srebrenica
SERBIA
Sarajevo
Pale
Mostar
MONTENEGRO
Pristina
Sofia
Dubrovnik
(Ragusa)
Titograd
KOSOVO
PROVINCE
BULGARIA
Kotor
Adriatic Sea
Roma
Skopje
MACEDONIA
Tirane
ALBANIA
GREECE

Juka Jaganjac & David Langworth

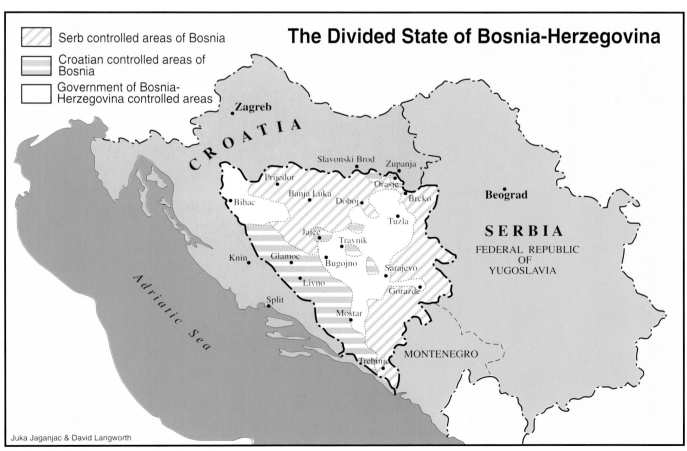

The Divided State of Bosnia-Herzegovina

Serb controlled areas of Bosnia

Croatian controlled areas of Bosnia

Government of Bosnia-Herzegovina controlled areas

Zagreb
CROATIA
Slavonski Brod
Zupanja
Prijedor
Orasje
Banja Luka
Doboj
Brcko
Bihac
Tuzla
Beograd
Jajce
Travnik
SERBIA
FEDERAL REPUBLIC
OF
YUGOSLAVIA
Knin
Glamoc
Bugojno
Livno
Sarajevo
Gorazde
Adriatic Sea
Mostar
Split
Trebinje
MONTENEGRO

Juka Jaganjac & David Langworth

Foreword
by General George A. Joulwan
Supreme Allied Commander, Europe

As the overall operational commander for both IFOR and now SFOR I applaud your efforts to do a follow-on to your excellent *IFOR on IFOR* publication. *The Road to Peace* tells the story in both pictures and words of the Stabilization Force. And it does so by the people themselves who have participated in this special mission to bring peace and stability to the people of Bosnia Herzegovina.

SFOR is a unique force. Thirty six nations co-operating together, training to common standards and procedures and working side-by-side with civilian agencies and non-governmental organizations! All working together as ONE TEAM — ONE MISSION. This time not to fight a war but to enforce and stabilize the peace in order for reconciliation and economic reconstruction to take place in Bosnia.

SFOR is breaking new ground in the history of Europe. There is now a Franco-German brigade in Bosnia. Ireland and Bulgaria have joined the Stabilization Force. Russian and NATO forces are conducting joint patrols and co-operating in Bosnia and their actions laid the foundation for the historic NATO-Russia Founding Act that ended the Cold War. SFOR now has reserves at the tactical, operational, and strategic levels. SFOR headquarters now consists of representatives from 25 nations — the most multinational headquarters in recent history.

General George A. Joulwan, SACEUR, at Tuzla airbase.

Therefore, *The Road to Peace* provides a timely reminder of what NATO and the international community can do in times of crisis. Your photos speak louder than words on our soldiers' compassion and sensitivity as well as their professionalism and readiness. Clearly success by SFOR will not only bring hope to the people of Bosnia, but also will establish a new security framework for Europe.

As the Supreme Commander for both IFOR and now SFOR it has been my privilege to command this special force. They do us all proud and the mission continues.

George Joulwan, SACEUR, Mons, Belgium
June, 1997

Opposite above:
A Bosnian girl smiles as a US Army Civil Affairs convoy pulls over. Brka village, near Brcko.

Opposite below:
Members of the Ukranian SFOR contingent, part of the French-German Brigade, walk across their base in Vrapcici, near Mostar. In the background are French Army vehicles.

Introduction

It wasn't until I played soccer with a bunch of schoolkids, a year after I first came to live in the country, that I really began to understand how things work in Bosnia. Our team of two adult aid workers and eight twelve year olds managed to hold together for just four evenings, playing well disciplined and energetic matches on the asphalt playground of Tusanj primary school in Tuzla. Eventually the kids got bored with our low standard of football and decided that hanging out with us was not cool. What became apparent was that the twelve year olds had a leader, a short charismatic blond guy called Alise (pronounced A-lee-say), with earings, a trendy haircut which flopped over his forehead, a purple and blue striped soccer shirt with the number six on the back and a cynical, understated attitude that somehow made everyone else obedient and respectful, including me. He was the unelected leader and without his nod the game would not commence. No explanation followed his refusal to condone the game but it was clear there was nothing I could do or say about it.

This helped me understand something fundamental about Bosnia. I realised that this whole society works in a similar way to what I had seen among my twelve year olds: each social unit has an unelected natural leader and what that leader says passes as law within that group. I was seeing Balkan society in miniature: leadership, fear of disobeying the leader, the leader's subtle way of giving orders and the total sense of acceptance. As a starting point to understanding the country, it helps if one sees Bosnia as a place that is ruled by leaders whose word is law. The large international community in Bosnia often come up against brick walls — simply because certain ethnic leaders do not give the nod.

Opposite:
A cat and a boat in an ancient street in Dubrovnik.

Below:
A group of young children in Tuzla.

The situation in Bosnia Herzegovina after the 1992-95 war is particularly confusing. On one level things are relatively good: the country is at peace; the seige of Sarajevo, the longest in the twentieth century, has ended; indiscriminate shelling of civilians has stopped; the armies have been demobilised and the weapons put away; normal economic and social life has started again. NATO, in the form of the Implementation Force (IFOR) and the Stabilization Force (SFOR) have done well in not only maintaining this peace but also in restoring the credibility of the international community following the dismal performance of the United Nations. The public utterings by the spokesmen for the international community are, on the whole, optimistic and the media are no longer interested in Bosnia.

On another level things look grim. The country that emerged from the peace talks held at Dayton, Ohio, in late 1995 was not a normal nation state with one government controlling all the territory, but a convoluted compromise between warring leaders who were forced to the negotiating table by economic hardship, international pressure and sheer exhaustion. Bosnia Herzegovina was subdivided into two entities: forty nine percent of the country under the Republika Srpska (the Bosnian Serb Republic) and fifty one percent to the Federation of Bosnia Herzegovina. Both of these entities have their own government, army, police force and economic policy. At the same time, both sides were obliged at Dayton to agree to the creation of a new central government of Bosnia Herzegovina made up of representatives from both entites. This extra layer of government is supposedly responsible for foreign policy, central banking, human rights and the constitution. Such an arrangement as this would be difficult to work anywhere in the world; but in Bosnia where one side simply refuses to deal with or tolerate the other, it is virtually unworkable. What keeps these central Bosnian institutions, as well as the whole peace process on track is the unflagging and optimistic determination of the international community to make it work.

To add further complexity to the situation, the two entities of Bosnia Herzegovina are deeply divided among themselves. The divide of hatred and mistrust that separates the Muslims from the Croats (the constituent partners of the Bosnian Federation) has been a well known feature of Bosnian political life since the United States forced a shotgun wedding between these two partners in 1994. The agreement that emerged in Washington DC that year did succeed in stopping the terrible war between the Muslims and Croats, forcing them to be uneasy allies against the more powerful Serb forces, but all the diplomatic muscle of the USA was unable to persuade the Croats to give up what has become their own mini-state within Bosnia: the Croat Republic of Herceg-Bosna.

If one travels to West Mostar, southern Herzegovina, or the small town of Orasje on the River Sava one comes across shops that only take Kuna (the Croatian currency), post offices that are part of the Croatian postal and telecommunication system, policemen in Croat uniforms, Herceg-Bosna number plates and the red chequerboard flag of Croatia flapping over the middle of main roads. These places are pieces of Croatian-run territory within Bosnia Herzegovina that officially do not exist. Bosnian Croats are even allowed to vote in Croatian elections. The international community, which favours Croatia and its highly developed western economy, choose not to comment on the fact that Croatia still controls a large part of another country. Today, relations are strained between the Croat leaders of Herceg-Bosna and the Muslim leaders of the remaining chunk of Bosnia Herzegovina. However, both sides know they are trapped in a marriage neither side wanted and fortunately both sides are interested enough in making money to realise it makes sense to co-operate with each other; keeping the trade routes open and paying lip service to the international community to ensure that the flow of reconstruction aid is not interrupted.

Opposite above:
A young girl peers inquisitively through the window of the photographer's car. Brcko.

Opposite below:
A potentialy booby trapped house lies abandoned in a field near Kladanj, central Bosnia.

The divisions within the Bosnian Serb Republic only burst into public view in mid 1997 when the split within their government became apparent. One look at the map shows that the Serb held territories are divided between large rural areas in the east and the west, both linked up by the narrow Posavina corridor in the north where the disputed town of Brcko is located. The only major city the Bosnian Serbs control is Banja Luka in the west, location of the Bosnian Serb Parliament and residence of the elected Bosnian Serb President, Biljana Plavsic. But the real power lies in the small eastern village of Pale (pronounced Pa-lay), a mountain resort not far from Sarajevo; this is where the government of the Bosnian Serb Republic operates, where government finances are controlled and where the indicted war criminal Radovan Karadzic lives.

The government of the Bosnian Serb Republic is deeply corrupt and Karadzic is reported to have millions of illegally earned dollars stashed away in Cyprus. He is widely suspected of still controlling the distribution of cigarettes and other goods in the Serb Republic and of still manipulating the government apparatus. The people on the western side of the Serb Republic are incensed by the fact that the Serbs in the village of Pale control and spend their national budget. Despite the Serbs' usual blind faith in their leaders their unity started to unravel in July 1997 when President Plavsic attempted to dissolve the pro-Karadzic Government. The government responded by denouncing her as a pro-western traitor. The Plavsic Banja Luka side of this divide have the support of the international community and the Bosnian Serb army, while the Pale side has the support of Serbian President Milosevic and the Bosnian Serb police force. The stage is set for a civil war between the Serbs and this is a real possibility in the next few years.

On top of these fragmented entities preside the representatives of the international community in the form of the Office of the High Representative (OHR). This organisation was created at Dayton by the Contact Group countries (France, Germany, Russia, UK and USA) who felt the peace agreement needed an agency that could supervise the civilian side of the agreement under the umbrella of security provided by NATO. The primary function of the OHR is to encourage the entity governments to set up the common institutions of Bosnia Herzegovina — the Joint Presidency, the Council of Ministers, the Parliamentary Assembly, the Constitutional Court and the Central Bank — thus enabling the country to function as a State and uniting the entity governments. Unfortunately every step of the way has been fraught with problems and endless delays. The Bosnian Serbs are the main stumbling block who, despite signing up for a unified Bosnia Herzegovina at Dayton, continue to block the reality of a united Bosnia. Their barely concealed plan is to break away from Bosnia Herzegovina and link up with Serbia proper; a plan that has already been partly achieved by the fact that Serbia and the Serb Republic already have a common currency, and phone system and to a casual visitor appear to be effectively the same country.

The OHR fight a ceaseless and largely unseen battle merely trying to facilitate meetings and physically bring the delegates together. The central institutions of Bosnia Herzegovina have been unable to work out the most basic arrangements such as opening telephone lines between the entities, agreeing on a common currency or a foreign policy. Until there is a sharp change in the attitudes of those people who lead the entities the likelihood of these common institutions working properly is very slim indeed. If the central institutions can not function the chance of Bosnia Herzegovina becoming a normal functioning state will remain unlikely under the present arrangement.

Living in Bosnia is actually quite pleasant. Despite the war and all the horrors that have gone on here it must not be forgotten that Bosnia was until recently part of a large and relatively prosperous country, Yugoslavia. This means that in most cities you can find a good apartment with tiled bathroom, central heating, satellite television, a telephone, washing machine, fridge and all the other conveniences one would expect at home. Despite this reality a lot of foreigners come to Bosnia thinking it will be like an undeveloped part of Asia or Africa where ancient ethnic hatreds have driven the people to fight each and people can hardly read. In fact the average Bosnian child receives a better education than the average American. Almost everywhere you go there are people who can speak your language and have a similar understanding of the world because they too have access to satellite TV and friends in other countries.

Despite all the trouble caused by the extremist politicians who want their ethnically pure mini-state, most Bosnians one meets on the Federation side simply want to live together as before, with the multi-ethnic neighbours they had before the war. It is actually quite hard to find an extremist, even on the Serb side, as everyone knows that the death and destruction caused in the name of ethnic supremacy has merely resulted in poverty for all. The lack of bitterness amongst ordinary people towards their ethnic opposite numbers is really astounding when one realises that this country has been divided up between politicians who want their piece of territory over which they can have absolute control.

In the final analysis it comes back to this question of leadership: the overwhelming majority of Bosnian people, be they Serb, Croat or Muslim, did not want a war and do not want another war in the future. But the ordinary Bosnians' opinion is irrelevant because what is overwhelmingly important are the views of the leaders of these three communities as it is they who decided to go to war in the first place and it is they who will decide whether or not to have another.

A bronze statue made during the communist era remains standing after fierce fighting between Serbs and Croats in 1992.

Trying to understand or make some sort of sense of Bosnia's war is essential for those visiting the country in any capacity, be they journalists, aid workers, or in the armed forces. Nor does it normally take the inquisitive visitor very long to realise that it happened as a direct result of Serbia's territorial ambition and then Croatia's realisation that it too could control large parts of Bosnia. If these two countries had respected the borders of Bosnia and Herzegovina when they were recognised by the United Nations and the European Union in 1992, there would have been no war.

This war, and most wars throughout the long history of Bosnia, happened as a direct result of the interference of neighbouring countries; it didn't happen as a result of ancient ethnic hatreds and the tendency for Bosnians to massacre each other every generation. Tito forbade the kind of inter-republic prejudice that he knew was a major threat to Yugoslavia and he punished Serb and Croat extremists particularly ruthlessly. Although the older generation of Yugoslavs, those who had suffered all sorts of brutalities at each other's hands during the First and Second World Wars, never forgot this inter-ethnic hatred, a new generation of post war Serbs, Croats and Muslims grew up and worked amongst each other, more conscious of their common Yugoslav identity than the brutalities their grandparents had witnessed.

The President of Serbia, Slobodan Milosevic, is seen as the man who personally orchestrated the collapse of Yugoslavia. A clever and wily political operator, he worked his way up through the Communist Party until he was in charge of Yugoslavia's destiny. Consisting of six republics (Slovenia, Croatia, Bosnia Herzegovina, Serbia, Montenegro and Macedonia) Yugoslavia became a volatile mix only when Milosevic's rabid Serb nationalism was allowed to poison the system. All through the late 1980s Milosevic was building up hatred among the Serb people against the Croats and Muslims. Messages of hatred, intolerence and revenge were communicated through the state controlled Serbian media and mass public rallies were held all over the country. The Serbs' hatred of the Muslims dates back to the Battle of Kosovo in the fourteenth century, when Serbia was finally defeated by the Turks. The Croats are equally hated because of the appalling massacres the Serbs suffered at the hands of the Ustache regime in the Second World War. At the same time the Communist regimes across Eastern Europe were collapsing like dominos, regimes that had seemed unchangeable were overturned at a pace that stunned the world. Although Yugoslavia's was not as rigid and orthodox as some of the other Communist regimes these events helped to de-stabilise the Yugoslav leadership that had already been weakened by the death of Tito.

By 1990 it had become clear that Serbia, the most populous of the republics, wanted to control all of Yugoslavia and through his personal control of the huge JNA (Jugoslav National Army) Milosevic was banking on the fact that the other republics would give in to him rather than face destruction. The Slovenians, the smallest and richest of the republics, first proposed a new confederation of republics in a reformed Yugoslavia. This was rejected by Milosevic who must have been outraged when they held a referendum and declared Slovenia an independent country. Within a year both Bosnia Herzegovina and Croatia had declared their own independent republics and all these new states were internationally recognised by the United Nations and the European Union.

Meanwhile Milosevic developed the Serb military option to such a degree that when the time came for war he was able to outmanoeuvre everyone. This was done very cleverly and in such a way that his invasion of Croatia and then Bosnia was made to look like a civil war between the various ethnic groups within each country. Milosevic's first military move was in 1991 when he deployed the JNA in Slovenia, but the Jugoslav army was poorly prepared at that stage, the Slovenians were better organised and highly motivated and within ten days the JNA withdrew.

In Croatia it was a different story as they had virtually no army and Serbia was more determined. In 1992 the JNA struck in three places simultaneously — the newly declared Serb Republic of Krajina in the middle of the country, Vukovar in the north east and Dubrovnik in the south west — and succeeded in cutting Croatia in two. Losing no time, Milosevic moved his columns into Bosnia Herzegovina and succeeded in conquering about seventy five percent of the territory and declaring it an autonomous Serb Republic. Far from being the Muslim fundamentalists of Serbian propaganda, the Bosnian Muslims had behaved with remarkable naivete and had made no preparations for the war that now engulfed them.

The newly elected President of Bosnia, Alija Izetbegovic, was so determined to avoid a war he disarmed the local defence brigades as a gesture of peaceful intent. As a result, the Serbian forces were able to literally walk into town after town in eastern, northern and western Bosnia and simply take over. It was only when the rumours of general massacres reached the stunned Bosnian Muslim and Croat leaders that they reacted accordingly and started to build up their armies.

What was particularly clever about Milosevic's method was how he managed to disguise his aggressive use of force and convince so much of the world that he was a

An abandoned street in the old quarter of Vukovar.

mere observer in a civil war that had somehow erupted of its own accord. Milosevic's use of force was well planned and he always covered his tracks with the expertise of a master burglar. A town would be selected for what has become known as ethnic cleansing — the genocide or expulsion of all non-Serbs in a community — and the Serbian war machine would move into action. The heavily armed JNA, officially in Bosnia on peace keeping operations, would fire heavy artillery into the town in order to soften up and frighten the population. Then the paramilitary forces, such as Arkan's Tigers and the White Eagles, would move in and deal with the population, driving out all non-Serbs from their houses and forcing them to leave the town instantly, on foot. Anyone who resisted would be executed on the spot. The houses were then robbed of all valuables which were sent back to Serbia as war booty.

Many of the local Serbs would be shocked at the behaviour of these ruthless paramilitaries and feel sorry for their Muslim and Croat neighbours, perhaps wishing to help them. But the sense of fear was so overwhelming and the paramilitaries worked with such brutal efficiency and speed that before long the newly dispossessed would be on their way, walking past those who had been publically executed as examples. The Serbs who remained would be implicated in these crimes by association, and by their inability to stop the injustice. This pattern of ethnic cleansing happened in huge areas of Bosnia Herzegovina, each time with the same ruthless efficiency. By the time the international community realised what was happening the paramilitaries and the JNA had gone back to Serbia, leaving their heavy weapons with a locally raised Serb Army that took up a more traditional military posture in the trench lines that then developed.

The interior of the Catholic cathederal in Vukovar after being destroyed by Serbian heavy artillery.

The bulk of ethnic cleansing took place in 1992 and by the end of that year the Serbs had occupied over three quarters of Bosnia, declaring their occupied territories an independent Serb Republic. Front lines that were then established between the opposing forces remained relatively static for the remainder of the war. By 1993 the international community had realised what was happening and the UN Protection Force (UNPROFOR) was sent in to help with humanitarian aid. Although UNPRO-FOR did not end the war they did help to focus the world's attention on the problem and freeze the Serbian gains, enabling the Croat and Muslim people a breathing space in which they could form armies and begin defending themselves. Following close on the coat tails of UNPROFOR came the international mediators, Lord Owen and Cyrus Vance. Their basic mistake was to deal with Milosevic as an equal, and not to condemn him as the aggressor, but take his proposal for dividing Bosnia into ethnically pure entities at face value. Scores of peace proposals were put forward but before the Dayton Peace Agreement few held for more than a matter of days; in fact the signing of a peace agreement was often the signal for fighting on the ground to intensify.

At the beginning of the war the Muslims and Croats had been fighting a common enemy, but by 1993 President Tudjman of Croatia realised that he too could carve out his chunk of Bosnia and for almost a year the Croats and Muslims fought bitterly against each other. By 1994 an uneasy truce had been put together between these two former allies and by 1995 the Croatian Army had become remarkably well equipped and the Bosnian Army had huge numbers of infantry. Operation Storm took place in mid 1995 and the Croatian and Bosnian Armies re-took a huge amount of Serb occupied territory in Croatia and Bosnia Herzegovina, the once powerful Serb Army

A mosque in the village of Amici, near Travnik in central Bosnia, destroyed during the bitter Muslim-Croat was of 1993 to 1994.

Above:
A stray dog looks out of an abandoned house onto the streets of Brcko.

Below:
An old Russian Lada with engine trouble is used as a hearse by a group of Bosnians.

putting up almost no resistence. These military successes against the Serbs coincided with the Americans becoming much more committed to finding a peaceful solution and by the end of 1995 the Dayton Peace Agreement had been signed and the war was effectively over.

1996 and 1997 will be remembered as years of peace in Bosnia Herzegovina, two years in which the international community poured enormous resources into stabilising the situation and creating a viable state that can continue a peaceful existence without such intense husbanding. There is no doubt that the active involvement of the United States has led directly to a cessation of conflict. But the peace that we are now enjoying is only skin deep because the injustices and war crimes that were committed against the people of Bosnia still remain unaccounted for and over a million people are still forbidden to return to their homes. The international community are here in force yet they have treated the former warring factions with kid gloves, dealing with regimes that are guilty of war crimes with the same politeness and neutrality as they deal with the representatives of the victims. In their neutrality the international community fail to distinguish between good and evil and this is a fatal mistake. To deal with a regime that is accused of genocide is to condone that regime and to postpone the inevitable resumption of war.

NATO's Stabilization Force (SFOR) is scheduled to pull out of Bosnia in 1998 and if this happens war will be a certainty. The Federation (Muslim-Croat) Army has been transformed by the Equip and Train Programme which is funded by the USA and the Islamic countries. This programme of officer training and importing heavy ordnance is aimed at bringing the Federation Army to a level with that of the Bosnian Serb Army and to create a balance of power that will theoretically prevent another war. According to the American ex-military trainers, the Bosnian officers are intelligent, enthusiastic, quick learners and the general consensus is that if there is another war it will be the Serbs who will be the losers this time.

In addition to these military reforms the economy on the Federation side is doing relatively well: houses are being rebuilt, new businesses are opening every day and in 1996 their economic growth rate grew by fifteen percent. In the Bosnian Serb Republic the growth rate was zero, there are very few cars on the roads, public employees haven't been paid in months and the army is deeply demoralised. Given the situation it is difficult to see how the NATO forces can just walk away when the SFOR mandate expires in June 1998, yet there is also a danger that this mission could drag on forever.

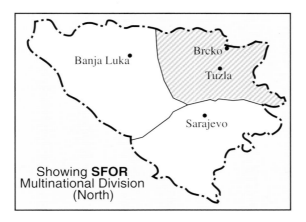

Showing **SFOR** Multinational Division (North)

Tuzla and northern Bosnia

Before the recent war the city of Tuzla was virtually unknown outside Yugoslavia and even within the country Tuzla's claim to fame was curious. From Macedonia to Slovenia people knew of the humorous folksong about how the whole city fed on the cheese of one goat. The song is about a law passed by the Austro-Hungarians (who ruled Bosnia from 1878 to 1918) which forbade Bosnians to keep domestic goats. So, officially there was only one goat in Tuzla and yet goat's cheese was still available in the market. The goat remains as a powerful symbol in Tuzla where the people are proud of their traditions of resistance as well as the ancient pedigree of their city.

Tuzla's coat of arms is an image of a boiling pan of salt, surmounted by the dates 976 and 1976. It refers to Tuzla's status as a salt town for the last thousand years. The town was named Tuzla during the Ottoman Empire, "Tuz" being the word for salt in the Turkish language. In modern times Tuzla was developed as an industrial city with a large salt mining industry, a chemical industry that used salt as raw material, and a huge power station fuelled by coal from the nearby mines. A university was built up to support these industries and by the time the war broke out Tuzla was a fully developed industrial city with an ethnically mixed population of over a hundred thousand people.

During the recent war Tuzla became famous for a number of reasons. It was here that the Serb-led JNA (Jugoslav National Army) suffered their first military defeat in 1992 at the hands of the Bosnians; a convoy of armoured vehicles and trucks was destroyed in a shoot-out with local police. The defence of Tuzla was organised by a committee representing all ethnic groups and the highly motivated Second Corps managed to stop the Serb advance in northern Bosnia and then win back a large area around Tuzla. By pushing the front lines away from the city, Tuzla was spared the terrible shelling and sniping that people in Sarajevo and Gorazde had to endure.

Opposite:
A member of the US Army First Infantry Division at Checkpoint Alpha One on Route Arizona; the road between Orasje and Tuzla.

The main reason Tuzla became so well known was because the mayor of the city, Selim Beslagic, was the only leader of a major Bosnian city who was not a member of a nationalist party. While Bosnia, as well as Serbia and Croatia, fell under the curse of nationalism, city after city came to be ruled by chauvinistic and intolerant leaders who sustained the inter-ethnic hatreds that helped keep the war going. As aid poured into Bosnia, representatives of the international community would visit the local leaders and look for like-minded partners through whom emergency aid and development funds would be safely delivered. Tuzla became a favoured destination for aid as it rapidly became clear that the city authorities were tolerant of all ethnic minorities and had a good economic development policy that has benefited the whole region.

Today Tuzla is booming. One indicator of its prosperity is the number of cars on the streets. It is remarkable to think that during the war there were no cars moving in the blacked out city and that now it is a problem finding somewhere to park. Trading is a major source of income as businessmen from all the entities take advantage of the open status of the city. As far as investment goes the emphasis is on developing small businesses rather than the huge factories that were set up by the Yugoslav state.

Thousands of jobs are provided by the international aid agencies that are based in Tuzla, a hundred and forty at the last count. These western agencies pay salaries that are usually three times the local average. The American SFOR base at Tuzla airport is the biggest employer in the area, with over a thousand local people working with engineering sub-contractors Brown and Root, the military-retail stores AAFES, and the translators' agency BDM. As a result Tuzla appears a lot more prosperous than most visitors expect from a city that has just emerged from a war.

A few miles south of Tuzla is a village called Dubrave. Situated in a wide, flat valley and flanked by impressive blue mountains, this was where the Yugoslavs built one of their main strategic military airbases in Bosnia, the others being in Sarajevo, Mostar and Banja Luka. It is a well built airbase with a two and a half kilometre runway, extensive buildings and reinforced concrete hangers hidden by trees. During the 1992-95 war it was utilised by the UN Protection Force (UNPROFOR) and after peace was finally agreed at Dayton in 1995, Tuzla airbase at Dubrave became the headquarters for the first American troops to be deployed in the former Yugoslavia.

The presence of the United States in Bosnia is critical to the peace process as no other country has the combination of huge air, ground and sea power, a powerful economic and population base and a massive logistical capability. As the war progressed, it became clear that the European powers lacked the will and capacity to end the conflict and the European powers put America under enormous pressure to send troops.

Despite the disapproval and indifference of Congress, the Republican Party and much of the American public, the US government committed itself to ending the war in Bosnia and by 1995 the decision to use air power and ground forces was taken. The Dayton Peace Agreement came about as a direct result of American diplomatic pressure and for as long as the US troops are stationed in Bosnia the peace is likely to hold.

Under NATO's Stabilization Force (SFOR) the US Army's First Infantry Division have approximately eight thousand troops in base camps around the Tuzla region, and a two star general with overall command of a multi-national NATO division. This US-led division consists of three American brigades and Russian, Scandinavian and Turkish brigades. The divisional area of operation covers about one third of Bosnia from the small town of Srebrenica in the east to the Sava River port town of Slavonski Brod in the north.

Above opposite:
The driver of a Humvee
checks his tyres at Camp
Demi, near Kladanj.

Below opposite:
An American trooper
waves to a group of
Bosnian Muslims who
are rebuilding their
houses in the disputed
Brcko suburb of Brod.

The curious thing about the Americans being in Bosnia is that war would not have ended were it not for their involvement, yet the American soldiers feel more vulnerable than the other SFOR troops. They are the most heavily protected and the most isolated from the local communities where they are based. It appears that President Clinton only managed to get Congressional approval to deploy troops by promising that there would be no American casualties. As a result the US commanders take no risks when it comes to the safety of their men and many soldiers say that it is in fact safer in Bosnia than it would be in many American cities.

With such restrictions, life in Bosnia for the ordinary American soldier is not easy. They are not allowed to leave their bases, the drinking of alcohol is forbidden in or out of camp, and they must eat, sleep and work with the same people every day for their full tour of duty — which can be up to nine months. Contact with local people is restricted to meeting the Bosnian staff who work as translators or cleaners on the bases. Consequently many of the soldiers get tremendously bored, not enough of them get the opportunity to go out on patrol and meet people, and some feel frustrated by the lack of real action. The sadness is that people in Tuzla see the Americans as saviours upon whose shoulders peace depends and they would welcome Americans into town.

The US Army is obviously a very reflective institution that studies its mistakes and adjusts accordingly. By looking at its history since Vietnam one can see how they have developed their cautious rules of deployment: in Vietnam the US backed one side against another and in the process lost over fifty thousand men; in Somalia they chased war criminals and the result was humiliation and withdrawal; in Japan some US servicemen were accused of rape and it became an international scandal; in Lebanon and Saudi Arabia the army was subject to terrorist attacks and ever since US Army posts abroad have been heavily guarded.

An SFOR Norwegian rifleman on duty at the tail end of a Finnish-built SISU Armoured Personnel Carrier.

Some critics feel that the US forces should go after the indicted war criminals, especially the notorious General Ratko Mladic who has his base in the US divisional area, but this is considered too risky an operation for American soldiers within a mission that is strictly neutral. In Bosnia all US soldiers have to wear a flak vest and helmet at all times, they must always carry a gun, and there must be a minimum of three armed vehicles when on patrol. As a result, the US forces are able to operate without incident, but at the same time the individual soldiers are deprived of the opportunity of getting involved in the local community.

The Scandinavians have fewer restrictions when it comes to dealing with the local community. Based in the small city of Doboj, an hour west of Tuzla, the Nordic-Polish Brigade consists of battalions from Sweden, Norway, Denmark and Poland, an engineering and infantry unit from Finland and individuals from Lithuania, Latvia, Estonia and Iceland. What is striking about meeting people from this unit is how well educated they are; most of the Scandinavian soldiers speak excellent English and they are professionals in the sense that back home they all have a civilian profession and they have volunteered for this peacekeeping mission in Bosnia. This gives a quality and intelligence to the brigade that is lacking in other units. Also, the Scandinavian equipment is highly regarded, in particular the Finnish-built SISU APC (Armoured Personnel Carrier).

As soldiers, the Scandinavians seem very alert and well trained and they have the advantage of being allowed to get involved in all sorts of charitable projects in the local community. Sweden and Denmark deployed troops in Bosnia during the war and Norway was the first to send troops to the Tuzla region when UNPROFOR (United Nations Protection Force) was set up in 1992. The Norwegian Medical Company ran a UN hospital in a blue painted building outside Tuzla all through the war and so well-known did this hospital become amongst the local people that the name 'Blue

A Bosnian civilian is scanned for concealed weapons by a member of the US Army First Infantry Division at Checkpoint Alpha One on Route Arizona.

Factory' has entered into the local laguage. In 1997 the Americans took over the Blue Factory medical facility and, ever since, local people have been denied access.

The Turkish Brigade are also involved in humanitarian projects. The city of Zenica, where they are based, has had all its churches and mosques rebuilt by Turkish soldiers. But the Turks are far less approachable than the Scandinavians and their general attitude to the SFOR mission appears to be one of doing things their own way, on their own. This is in sharp contrast to the Nordic-Polish Brigade whose headquarters is made up of soldiers from Nordic and ex-Communist countries. However, the Turks have one of the largest armies in Europe as well as a lot of combat experience and as a result their SFOR brigade is fully self sufficient with infantry, armour and engineers and their need to rely on other units is perhaps less.

The soldiers of the Russian Parachute Brigade, located in the north east corner of Bosnia, are as aloof as the Turks. This is partly due to the fact that very few of the Russians speak other languages and also because they are proud and somewhat inexperienced at dealing with people of other nationalities. However, if you can break through this Russian reserve and be accepted into their group you will find their friendliness so intense and passionate that it will leave a deep impression.

Relations between the American and Russian SFOR brigades appear to have been very good so far. The novelty of this first joint mission since the Second World War is such that the US commanders take great pleasure in dealing with the Russians. However, this camaraderie at brigade level disguises the deep differences between the Russian and American governmental positions on Bosnia Herzegovina. The Kremlin is a traditional supporter of Serbia and openly supports the Bosnian Serb Republic; the Pentagon, on the other hand, is one of the main advocates of a united Bosnia Herzegovina and openly supports the Croats and Muslims.

This cordial relationship between the two superpowers will remain stable for as long as SFOR keeps its mandate very strictly limited: inspecting arms dumps, monitoring the ceasefire line, separating the forces and helping the civilian agencies with security and logistics. But if SFOR commits itself more deeply to one side or another, or starts hunting Serbian war criminals, this fragile American-Russian friendship could disintegrate very quickly.

Opposite above:
US Army MP gives his highly-trained sniffer dog a drink of mineral water.

Opposite below:
A US soldier on patrol in Brcko shortly after the 1997 arbitration decision failed to settle the status of this disputed town.

US Army Interviews

Dwight Anderson
Command Sergeant Major,
1–18th, 1st Infantry Division.
Interviewed at Camp McGovern, Brcko.

Dwight Anderson, second from right, poses with SFOR commander Colonel Steve Layfield (second from left) and others at Camp McGovern near Brcko.

"In the little town where I grew up there were two places you could drink your beer, the pub and the Canadian Legion. All my heroes drank their beer down at the Legion. There was never any question of what I wanted to do — I wanted to be a soldier. I was young and looking for adventure and it's kind of hard convincing a sixteen year old that he can't live forever.

Canada wasn't involved in Vietnam and even at sixteen I felt Communism should be opposed so, at eighteen years old, I emigrated to the United States and joined the US Marine Corps. I served twenty one months as an infantryman and spent a year in Vietnam, that was 1969. I was lucky to be wounded only one time — shrapnel in the back of my head, leg and hand — from a booby trap. I went to Vietnam with thirty two Marines and at the end of twelve months there were only six of us who weren't either killed or badly maimed, and of those six we had been wounded ten times between us. It wasn't very positive coming back to America, we got tomatoes and eggs thrown at the bus right outside the airport. I checked out and went back to Canada and got a job in a mine.

I then went to the west coast and got a job in a Norwegian tramp freighter, travelled all over and ended up in Norway where I learned the language and got a job in a plastics factory. I returned to Canada and worked on oil rigs in the Arctic, then with a Norwegian Luxury Cruiser as a deck steward, going on cruises to the Carribean, South Africa — all over the world.

On the 30th of April 1974 I joined the US Army as an infantryman. I always knew I wanted a military career but right after Vietnam I wasn't ready for it and I certainly wasn't going to stay in the Marine Corps. So I saw the world. Coming here to Bosnia is my seventy ninth country.

The Army's been very good to me. I went from private to Command Sergeant Major in seventeen years. I'm responsible for discipline and morale in the battalion, the advisor to the commander for all enlisted matters, run the training programmes and conduct the promotion boards. I like to get involved in the training side of things because I understand both sides of the house pretty well.

I was taken aback by the devastation in Bosnia. I knew there was World War One style fighting here but I wasn't prepared for the devastation. Even Vietnam, which was pretty destroyed, wasn't anything like this.

I've read the history of the Balkans and I don't believe this war was because of their history. I believe the people here were victims of Communist aggression from Serbia, and Milosevic used Serbian nationalism to further his goals. We made a mistake when we first came in here because we didn't go and pick up the war criminals — as we did in Nazi Germany after World War Two. We sanitised Germany of its Nazis. But this hasn't happened here. War criminals are living openly, many still in positions of power, and I really don't believe the healing process can take place unless the people who committed the war crimes are taken care of.

It's not SFOR's mission to do that but I believe it should have been. You only have to grab the first few and the rest will book steerage on tramp freighters and head for Argentina, I'm sure they've got plans to escape. As long as Radovan Karadzic, Milosevic and a lot of these characters are running around the healing process won't be able to begin.

I think that under our Task Force, Brcko has been a real success story. The goodwill that we're able to generate between the leaders on all three sides has been remarkable. The local people could easily resolve this Brcko problem, if only their leaders above them could stay out of this.

Pale (the capital of the Serb Republic) would like to put some hard core Serbs in here, people they don't need to teach how to hate Muslims. Along what we call the 'biological line' (between the Serbs and Muslims), people are starting to talk to each other, to interact. The goodwill that the ordinary people have for each other will ultimately be their salvation. That is my hope and belief.

A member of the First Infantry Division Civil Affairs team speaks with a village farmer near Brcko.

Because Americans move around so much it was hard for us to understand why the Bosnians want to return to their beat up homes, but since I've got to know this old

couple that I take food and clothing to — she was injured in a mine accident and lost her foot — it has become clear to me why they are so intent on returning to their homes. She said that during the war she moved nine times, and since the war ended she's had to move at least twice. All she wants to do is return to her home. It may be bombed, it may look like hell but they can fix it up.

The people here have left a great impression on me. I've really come to know and to love them. The stories you hear about the people fighting back against Arkan's Tigers and the JNA (Jugoslav National Army), fighting back with shotguns and rifles and Molotov cocktails and grenades, are truly heroic. I have met people who are Gold Lily winners, that's their equivalent of the Medal of Honor; young guys of twenty years old who have destroyed four tanks, six tanks, one guy seventeen tanks. These guys are legends in the area and my hat is absolutely off to them. It's awe inspiring how long they were able to defend their homes and families and in the end had IFOR not come in, if we had let them go on a few more months, they would have reclaimed the country because they were certainly winning by the end. The Serbs' hearts weren't in it once the JNA went home.

If I were to make a prediction it would be this: if we leave in 1998, and totally keep our hands off this place, the Bosnian Army will attack and re-take what is now Republika Srpska. The Bosnians have been rearming with M-60 tanks, with M-113s, M-16 rifles, our artillery, and the majority of hard core soldiers are refugees who see the Bosnian Army as a way of reclaiming their village or house. Left to their own that's what I believe will happen. I really see that coming.

This country is very unique to Europe. If you look at the history and culture of Bosnia you see that it is composed of Muslim, Catholic and Orthodox religions. They have been together through the centuries and to me this is unique. Bosnia ought to be preserved as a country; it would be a shame if part of Bosnia were to be torn away by Croatia and part by Serbia and you were left with a little rump Muslim Federation. But then I'm reminded of the nursery rhyme:

Humpty Dumpty sat on the wall
Humpty Dumpty had a great fall
All the King's horses and all the King's men
Couldn't put Humpty together again.

And here we are; we're the King's horses and the King's men, and we'll see if we can do it. There are a lot of lessons to be learned from Bosnia.

Look at Germany and the events leading up to the Second World War; I don't believe the Germans are a bad people with a genetic defect that causes them to start goose-stepping every twenty years. They were victims of the Versailles Treaty, their middle class was wiped out and suddenly the people on the bottom were on the top and when these people got into positions of power they were able to act out their prejudices.

Every society has their little Hitlers. What happened here was that the bad people managed to overcome the good ones and this terrible war took place. There's lessons here for America. Look at the Oklahoma city bombing. Look at the militia groups. Then you ask yourself what kind of people could do the crimes that were committed here in Bosnia? But then we realise that those same people, that same mentality, exists in America and if conditions were right those militia groups and the hate groups could create another Bosnia, they could do in America what they've done in Bosnia.

You have to be aware that this element exists in every society and if they can get the upper hand they will act out their hatred, they will act out their prejudices. That's the real lesson of Bosnia, not that Bosnians are bad people who have been fighting each other for five hundred years and will go on fighting each other, but that events allowed things to get out of hand. To me it typifies the struggle between good and evil — sometimes evil gets the upper hand."

Bosnian Serb children around a US "Humvee" in the garrison-town of Han Pijesak, current home to indicted war criminal General Ratko Mladic.

Lieutenant William Wilburn Honea
82nd Airborned Division.
Liaison Officer to the SFOR Russian Parachute Brigade.
Interviewed at Camp Dobol.

American and Russian SFOR soldiers share a joke at their joint checkpoint near the northern Bosnian village of Celic.

"I come from the western part of Alaska and the profession I grew up with was commercial fishing. Although I was earning good money I feel everyone should serve his country in some capacity and I wanted to join the army. When I was growing up in Alaska there were a lot of Russian fishermen there. After the Russian Revolution a lot of religious groups left the Soviet Union, fearing religious persecution, and they ended up in Alaska forming their own little communities. I interacted with them and learned from them.

Then I went to University and studied International Relations and Russian. Part of the course included a year's study in Moscow. I was there from 1991 to 1992 which was the moment when Communism was falling apart, a really interesting time. I studied hard for the first six months, I was a good student and went to classes every day. But then the school started falling apart, the teachers weren't getting paid and so I started travelling. I spent a month in the Caucases, another month in Central Asia — Turkmenistan, Uzbekistan, Kazakhstan — and there's still so much to see.

I love Russia. It's like America in lots of ways although this is more of a feeling than anything else. It's a big country and the people have big opinions of not only themselves but also of their national capabilities. Despite the fact that we were enemies throughout the cold war there are a lot of similarities between us. They don't like to be second to anyone, they like things big, and they are very open, straightforward, friendly.

Part of the reason why I joined the army was that I figured my father and grandfather would look down their noses at me if I didn't joined and I didn't want to be fifty years old and thinking, 'I wish I had join the military'. I'm in the 82nd Airborn Division, based at Fort Bragg with the 504th Parachute Infantry Regiment. I was lying in bed one morning after a field exercise when the phone rang and my boss said to me, 'Do you want to go to Bosnia as a Russian Liaison Officer?' A week later I was on a plane to Bosnia.

Working with the Russians here reminds me of my impressions of the US Military fifty years ago, just after World War Two. Very self contained, self reliant, not a lot of logistics. Here's an example: When we went into the town of Dugi Dio, a joint operation with US Forces providing security for the east side of the town and the Russians the west side, the US came in with a massive procession of vehicles: tanks, trucks, Bradleys. The Russians came in with one truck and a BTR (an Armoured Personnel Carrier). The BTR parked, the truck backed up, the soldiers got out.

These were the guys I was going to be living with for three weeks and I was a bit nervous about it. We were all living in the mud and they just had one tent. The US

Opposite above:
An infantry foot-patrol in Brcko.

Opposite below:
Two American soldiers take a break from foot patrolling in Brcko.

The boot of a Russian paratrooper laid out to dry on a BTR-80 Armoured Personnel Carrier. Near Ugljevik.

guys had everything they needed, stacks of food, water, timber. The Russians gathered old bricks, made flooring, they scavenged up a bunch of rocks and they made a sidewalk. They dug trenches all round, they dug a toilet and a bathroom and they had a little water heater and a stove. A truck would come three times a day and give them kasha, a type of porridge, and we would eat that with bread and soup. They are not reliant on a big logistic backup. Their army is considerably different.

That was a good time living with the Russians at Dugi Dio. Typically what I do is go with a platoon that is working with the Russians and one of my main duties is facilitating trade, being a broker. The US guys want to trade — a Leatherman for a fur hat, a knife for a Russian beret — but they can't talk to each other. Everyone wants to go home with a souvenir.

Being at Jusici (a village in the Russian sector) was intensely boring, but that's the way of the military — a great deal of boredom punctuated by a few interesting moments or, in war, a few moments of terror. You get a different perspective when you are completely isolated from your own countrymen for a while, you develop an affinity for those you are with. Obviously you need to keep a perspective of who you're working for. You can lose sight of that. I'm not a member of the Russian Airborne Brigade, I'm a member of a US Airborne Division. Occasionally you have to remind yourself of who you're working for.

I think the mission here has been more succesful than anyone had initially expected. Since this operation started there has been less violence here than in any major

A Bosnian-Serb refugee child greets an American soldier in the notorious town of Srebrenica

US city. The death rate for soldiers is less than in a typical US Army post just from drinking and driving. From that perspective it's been immensely succesful. From the perspective of the people of this country, and if they really want peace and want to resolve their differences, that's something that's just going to take time. You can't go from a massive level of violence they had here to, 'Okay, we'll be friends and neighbours again', just overnight. It takes time. I think realistically this mission is a much longer mission than two or three years. But this doesn't depend on my opinion, but on the American people and voters and those a lot higher than me.

As far as my perspective goes the most important thing is our relationship with the Russians. I can remember as a little kid watching those Doomsday movies, World War Three, NATO, Warsaw Pact, nuclear weapons. I can remember being terrified of nuclear war between Russia and the USA. When you look at the relationship between Russian and the USA today and the expansion of NATO coming up as a major strategic issue, this is the only positive thing going on between the Russian and US militaries, in fact it's the only thing going on and I think a lot of the time you can lose sight of just how critical our relationship is. After all Russia is still the only nuclear superpower, apart from the United States, however bad its economic situation may be."

Jim Shanks
**Sergeant. 364th MPAD
(Mobile Public Affairs Detachment).
Interviewed at Camp Dobol.**

"I was mobilised to come out to Bosnia Herzegovina and I had very little time to sort my affairs out. I was renting out a room in my house to a person and I gave him notice to move, because I was coming here. He committed suicide in my house, blew his brains out.

Two days later the tax office called and said they were going to seize my property for back taxes. At work they fired my boss and gave me his job, a job I had never done before. I had to find someone to take care of my house and my cat. I have a limousine business and own five cars; I had to find places to put all those. It was a scramble to get all this organised in a week and a half.

There are eighteen people in my unit — they're creative, a different breed — we have to find stories for the military press and AFN (American Forces Network). My main drawback is having to wear a flakvest and carrying two hundred and ten rounds of ammunition, a rifle, a tripod, a camera, a helmet and still try to get a good shot without stepping on any landmines. I still haven't got used to having showers in a trailer, wearing the same uniform seven days a week, working sixteen hours a day. I think I'm slowly going mad.

A US soldier on escort duty gets back into his "Humvee" vehicle at Celic; every American convoy is protected by this type of weapon. The mosque in the background has been recently renovated.

Sometimes I set up the camera and people talk into it and send the cassette home. A lot of families back home don't have a clue why we are out here. I didn't until I got here. I know it's pretty scary for the soldiers; wives are missing them, kids are going through types of phobia. I miss my home, but I miss my bathroom the most. I don't have to listen to other people snoring at home, there's no mud in my home and I drive nice cars, not a dusty old Hummer.

On the way down here we were passing through Austria and we stopped at a fuel station, all the buses lined up and we got out. There was this big guy standing there and he was shouting at me, he wanted to speak to me. It turned out he'd been in the French Foreign Legion and he'd been injured by a hand grenade. Right in the middle of the parking lot he dropped his trousers and showed me his scar. I didn't know what I was supposed to do, show him mine?

The most memorable thing here is seeing all the children, how similar they are to American children, what a great attitude they have, how they just want to play, to fit in. They're unscathed by all that's going on around them, they've accepted all this death and destruction as the norm.

I think a lot of innocent people are going to be killed again. There are a lot of hidden agendas amongst the politicians here. It's as if they're in suspended animation right now. We try to introduce the notion of accepting the other person and they are going through the motions. I think that when we do leave, and I hate to say this, but I think that it will all start over again. I just hope it's not on the calibre of last time with horrific mass murder and torture, rape and everything else that went on here."

First Infantry Division soldiers walk across the Brcko bridge towards Croatia.

The Nordic-Polish Brigade
Interviews

Gunnar Lundberg
Brigadier, Norwegian Army
Commander of Nordic-Polish Brigade, Doboj.
Interviewed in Doboj.

"When I was growing up in Norway after the Second World War there was a lack of everything. One could find evidence of the war everywhere, all through my youth, including dead bodies. Lots of our towns had been completely destroyed by German bombers and food was rationed for many years after 1945. I decided this must never happen again and for that reason I joined the armed forces.

Norway was one of the founding members of NATO. We joined on the 4th of April 1949, NATO's start date. We received lots of help from the USA — the Marshall Plan and a supply of weapons up to the 1960s — and then we discovered oil and have since become a rich country. Although there are no permanent NATO bases in Norway, that was a trade off with the Soviet Union, every year we take NATO troops for winter training. The British Royal Marines have been training in Norway since the 1960s.

On the Bosnian Serb side there is a split community between those who want peace, people who say, 'we used to live together before and we can live together again but the stupid politicians will never allow us to', and those who could never in their wildest imagination consider living with their Muslim and Croat neighbours again. The local people don't seem to be interested in politics, just survival.

The Federation side want a united Bosnia but Republika Srpska (the Bosnian Serb Republic) has officially declared that the Serb areas are for Serbs only, and they have signed a treaty with Serbia formalising this. The Serbs did sign the Dayton Peace Agreement but they object to Annex Seven which allows refugees the right to return home. The Bosnian Serbs say they will consider refugees being compensated, or properties being exchanged but they don't recognise the individuals' right to return. They say they can only live with the Muslims if there is a border between them. Is a looser federation of Bosnia-Herzegovina worth considering?

The people here have inherited the Communist system and the ruling parties, on both the Republika Srpska and Federation side, command their people, telling them

Brigadier General Gunnar Lundberg, commander of the SFOR Nordic-Polish Brigade, Doboj.

A Norwegian SISU Armoured Personnel Carrier follows a Yugoslav-made Zastava car through the Serb-controlled town of Modrica.

what is and what isn't allowed. The people accept this from the Communist Party days when government was very centralised and you couldn't do anything without permission.

Last year the Federation side recorded a fifteen percent growth and the Serb side none. If this continues there's a reason for the Serbs to fight, nothing has improved for them. I'm afraid that if we leave in 1998 with the map in the the same position there's going to be a big risk of war, the international community will lose credibility and will not be able to come back.

I don't think the mission could survive without American firepower and the credibility that the small European countries just don't have. The USA is the superpower behind this mission. I have two hundred and forty Americans just supporting this brigade with heavy artillery. But it will be hard for Scandanavians to leave this country without finding a peaceful solution. It's against our nature."

Mart Pella
Sergeant First Class,
Swedish Airborne Rangers.
Interviewed at Camp Oden.

"I live in the forest, six kilometres from a village called Nykvarn and two kilometers from the nearest neighbour. There is a lake in front of our house. I have always lived there. Growing up in such a place was one of the most perfect things you could do, I never wished we had lived nearer to the city. I was never lonely and I have never had problems getting to know people. At school people would say, 'Isn't it boring?' but my brother and I had so many friends. Whenever we went into the forest, hunting, hiking or out in the boat I always had friends with me. I got a motorbike two years earlier than was allowed and I would ride it through the forest and then get the bus into town. Stockholm, the capital of Sweden, is only forty minutes away.

My father is from Estonia. In 1945 he was a refugee escaping from the Russians. He and his mother managed to get away while one of his brothers was drafted into the German army and one was forced into the Russian army. Neither of them wanted to fight each other and both of them ran away. Their stories are incredible. My father became an officer in the Swedish Airborne Rangers and it happened that I came to fulfil my father's dreams for his son by also managing to get into the Airborne Rangers.

I was twenty two when I joined the army, before that I had been studying Industrial Technology at university and doing summer jobs at Scania. When I was in the army, Scania called me and asked me if I was interested in a full time job with them. This was in 1992 when jobs were hard to find and I thought I should get my foot in the door. I said I would join for one year only but I had all these expensive interests — climbing, diving, parachuting — so I stayed another year and ended up staying five. Scania is one of the most advanced companies in the world in terms of industrial management techniques and we have visitors from all over the world studying how we work and how we think.

I thought there would be a lot more trouble in Bosnia. On the news you only see the worst things. I didn't think it would be so beautiful, the people so open towards us. I thought it would be hostile, I had no idea that people would appreciate us as much as they do. They are pleased that we are here, always happy to see us, and that feels good. I think the Bosnians still have a lot of problems to sort

Above:

First Class Sergeant
Mart Pella of the
Swedish Airborne Rangers,
at Camp Oden, south of
Tuzla.

out, although I think the rest of the world thinks everything is okay here because the war is over. But is six months enough to see what's really going on here? It takes a month just to get into it, and that's after lots of training on history, religion, culture, how to behave. And just as you're starting to get a hold on it — you're going home.

I think the reason for the war was political and economic and the religious motive certainly wasn't the main reason. Everyone we talk to says they don't care if there's a Muslim or a Croat or a Serb living next door. They have been living and working all over the former Yugoslavia. They often tell us they have been working for ten or fifteen years with the different ethnic groups on a railway or down a mine. I think religion is just an excuse used by the leaders and the media to justify all that they have done. Many people say they're able to live as neighbours, others not, but often it depends on what happened to their families during the war. Many people say that the war is going to come back as soon as we leave.

Every day people in the villages tell me that the war isn't over until the people who were expelled are going to get their land back. It's hard for us to understand but these people see getting their land back as all important. It doesn't matter if we support them or not because they will always count on going home, even if it's a single family going back to a village where they will be in a minority.

In Sweden the young refugees from the former Yugoslavia say their parents all want to go home, but they don't. They have learned the language and made friends while the parents are still longing for the life they knew. As long as there's just one voice saying he wants to go home there will be problems, maybe that person is a good speaker and can influence other people.

Opposite:
A Bosnian woman carries water from a communal source to her recently rebuilt home near Doboj. Note the Swedish SFOR Armoured Personnel Carrier in the background.

Below:
A Bosnian man walks his cow to a pasture in a village near Gracanica; a Swedish machine-gun partially blocks the view.

Previous spread:
A Bosnian Muslim
shopkeeper explains how
his community managed
to reclaim their village
which is located in the
Serb-held hills above
Doboj.

I often say to myself that I will never complain again about water, food, getting bread, things that make the day more normal. Here they need each other and in the villages you can see that everyone's helping each other — to get the road fixed, the electricity line installed, the phone lines working. The last thing they are in need of is another war. I can imagine how many steps back the war has put them.

Once I asked a villager what he thought SFOR should do to keep the peace here: keep an eye on the local troublemakers; keep an eye on the weapons; or if the American Equip and Train Programme will help to stabilise the situation and separate the parties. He said it was the show of force — both sides know that if they start something we would strike them. This was a forty year old villager speaking, he seemed to be well informed and he felt sure that the day SFOR leaves is the day that war will start again. It's simply us being here that makes the difference.

All this has given me a fake picture of peace; it's not real peace, it's peace because we are here. That made me realise that when we go from here we will only have helped people from day to day, maybe the young girl will be a bit older but the buildings they are repairing will be destroyed again."

Dennis Thorensen
2nd Reconnaisance Platoon,
Danish Army. Interviewed near Doboj.

A member of the Danish
Recconnaisance Platoon
walks in front of his
convoy in order to detect
anti-tank mines. Ozran
pocket, near Doboj.

"I joined the army because it fascinated me. I trained in the Danish Navy Seals and it was very hard. We trained for long distance patrols on land and sea and we also did underwater patrols. I have served here before, covering all of central Bosnia during the war here. It was exciting. We weren't peacekeepers and we weren't peacemakers, we were something in the middle.

My best experience in Bosnia, the time I felt most useful, was in a small town that had a mental hospital that had been abandoned by its staff. We stayed in that hospital for eight days and took care of all three hundred and eighty people. They had no food or water and we improvised.

Under UNPROFOR (United Nations Protection Force) the local people were hostile towards us, they would shout at us and throw stones. Now, when people wave at us I do not wave back because I remember the war and how there were checkpoints everywhere. You couldn't go anywhere and they would stop you whenever they wanted.

The people in Sarajevo weren't particularly involved in the war but they were surrounded by the war. A lot of the snipers were from Serbia, and other countries. Sarajevo was a closed city, nobody could leave and this suited the snipers. I saw them kill small children of three or four years old, old men and women, UN troops. They didn't care.

Our mission here is to to keep the peace and to keep the parties separated. Our actual job here is to control the police as they are the bad guys now, always provoking the other parties. It's looking bad in Bosnia at the moment because as soon as we pull out they'll be fighting again, but it's difficult to see who is strongest now. They still hate each other. It's a beautiful country, it's a pity they're wrecking it."

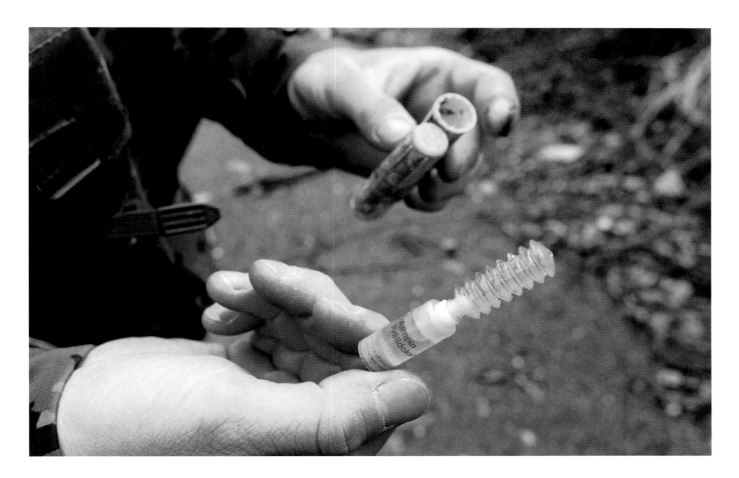

A capsule containing the antidote to nerve gas; the plastic tip contains a syringe that must be stabbed into the heart in the event of a gas attack. The presence of these antidotes, discovered by a member of the Danish SFOR contingent in Bosnian-Serb held areas, suggest that the Serbs have quantities of nerve gas in stock.

A view of central Brcko, US Army checkpoint and Serb flag.

POLICING THE POLICE
International Police
Task Force Interview

To anyone who does not follow Bosnia closely, the small market town of Brcko (pronounced birch-co) is unknown and unpronounceable. To the international community and the former warring parties Brcko is one of the most critical places, if not *the* most critical place, on the post-Dayton map of Bosnia Herzegovina. In Spring 1992, during the early stages of the war, Brcko was seized by Serbian irregular forces backed up by the heavy artillery of the Serb-dominated Yugoslav National Army. The non-Serb local inhabitants fought bravely but were soon pushed out. Large numbers were massacred by the Serb irregulars and buried in mass graves.

The strategic location of Brcko cannot be overstated. To the Bosnian Serb Government it is a vital point on the narrow corridor that connects their east and west territories; they cannot afford to lose it. To the Muslim-Croat Federation, Brcko was an important example of a multi-ethnic town and under the Dayton Agreement thousands of Muslim and Croat refugees are scheduled to return home. However their return has been blocked by Bosnian Serb police and local officials who carry out an unofficial policy of intimidation.

Brcko is also a key trading entrepot for Bosnia's traditional heavy industries of coal, salt and steel. It has Bosnia's main export port on the River Sava and key road and rail lines go through the town. The Sava is linked to the great Danube-Rhine river route. Just north of Brcko are large railyards and a Yugoslav-built motorway linking Zagreb with Belgrade. Because of this location Brcko was formerly the richest town in Bosnia.

In recognition of its strategic importance, the international community gave Brcko its own section in the Dayton Agreement: Annex two, Article five. Brcko was the one area where compromise proved impossible and the decision on whether the Serbs or the Federation were to control the town was postponed. An Arbitration Board was set up to make this impossible decision but their eventual conclusion, which was to be "final and binding" according to the Dayton Agreement itself, was to postpone the decision until March 1998.

In 1997 the international community, desperate to find a solution for this town, set up special offices in Brcko. A so-called "supervisor" of the Arbitration Board was installed under the auspices of the Office of the High Representative (OHR); an expanded IPTF (International Police Task Force) operation was set up under Don Grady; and Madeleine Albright was flown in to open the bridge link with Croatia. In the midst of all this diplomatic activity the IPTF have to go about their everyday business of training, advising and monitoring the local police in democratic police practices. In normal circumstances this task would be routine, especially with the motivated people that IPTF have recruited, but a more hard-line and uncompromising police force than that of the Bosnian Serb Republic would be hard to find anywhere.

In addition to these problems the IPTF is burdened with a typically unworkable UN Mandate: No executive authority over the local police force; their police officers come from over twenty countries so levels of professionalism vary wildy; IPTF officers are unarmed and located in remote areas, unable to prevent crime, investigate abuse or do anything other than observe and report. One of their main roles is to report on human rights abuses, many of which might otherwise have been unreported. At worst they are sitting targets for extremist groups, liable to be kidnapped and held ransom in retaliation for the international community arresting war criminals.

The following interview with Don Grady, chief of the IPTF operation in Brcko, stopped me in my tracks and continues to fascinate me every time I read it. It is a reminder that there are some exceptional people working in Bosnia.

A US Army foot-patrol through downtown Brcko.

Don Grady
District Commander for Brcko Special District.
IPTF (International Police Task Force).
Former Chief of Police of Sante Fe,
New Mexico, USA. Interviewed in Brcko.

Don Grady,
Commander of IPTF
Brcko Special District.

"My earliest memories of the police are very good. We had an officer who we called Moose. We would be out playing basketball and Moose would drive up in his squad car, get out, take his gunbelt off and shoot buckets with us. He was a very nice guy. If there was something going on and he wanted to know we would tell him, because Moose was the kind of guy who was interested in what was going on.

But as I grew older my recollections of the police changed considerably. I know of people who were beaten and abused by police officers; this is not something you just read about in stories, it's real. I know these people, I saw the injuries, but if you talk to the police they tell you he fell down the stairs, he accidentally bumped into the door.

At one point in my life I thought I was going to be a rock and roll star, and I looked the part: I had a mohawk that was three inches off the top of my head, I wore platform shoes, I was six foot five and weighed two hundred and twenty pounds. It was one o'clock in the morning, in a town in Wisconsin that's all white, and I was walking back from the drummer's house when I got stopped by two squad cars full of police officers.

They threw me up against the hood, put a gun to my head, patted me down and said I matched the description of an armed robbery suspect they were looking for. As I'm draped across the hood of the car the description of the armed robbery suspect comes over the air: two white males, average height five foot ten, about a hundred and seventy pounds, blond hair and blue eyes. How on earth did a six foot five black male fit that description?

My opinions on policing vary radically from what you'll find in the normal police culture. Once I became part of the system it became clear to me that it's a very strong, solid culture that's being perpetuated. So over the years I've developed philosophies and ideas about what we should be doing.

If you ask ten different police chiefs what Community Policing is you'll get ten different answers. I say it doesn't matter what the Chief of Police thinks Community Policing is, what matters is what the community thinks it is. What we've done over the years is eliminate the most important part of the police function: the community. They're the ones who should be telling us what they need.

We have to look at the individuals in the community and find out what their wants and needs are. As police officers what we generally do is decide, unilaterally, what's good for the community and then do it. The police need to begin to listen. We don't listen and we don't ask questions.

If we were a business we would be focused on consumer needs. If you don't look at the consumer and work out how to provide a service that either meets or exceeds your expectations, you go out of business, you go bankrupt. Policing is the one profession where I don't have to meet any of your needs or expectations — and you'll still give me a raise and more staff. There's a paradox here that shouldn't exist.

In 1829 Robert Peel said, and I paraphrase, 'the true measure of police organisation cannot be found in their ability to catch criminals after a crime has been committed, but in their ability to prevent crime.' Now, if we see crime prevention as the hallmark of good policing then clearly we have a greater obligation to work towards that goal than merely trying to arrest and apprehend after the fact.

We've been putting our resources in the wrong place, we've been focusing on one particular aspect of policing — Law Enforcement — and never done it particularly well. By focusing entirely on Law Enforcement we provide a tremendous disservice to the population. That needs to be changed, not just in America but worldwide. We have to be astute enough to recognise that the real responsibility of policing is to help build a community.

Most officers get into policing right after High School. College degrees are discriminated against by some Police Departments, they want the High School graduates. That means all my socialising up to that point has been with adolescents, and now I'm part of a very tightly knit social group. Once I'm a police officer I only go out with other police officers; I cut off all socialising with everybody else. That's how the us-versus-them attitude gets perpetuated.

We need to educate our officers. It doesn't take a rocket scientist to work out that if you're a High School graduate and you haven't spent any time figuring out Human Rights, what those rights are and how you go about preserving them, how do you make sure you don't violate someone's Human Rights? If you've done a class in legal matters that only lasts a couple of weeks how do we expect you to retain all that information and be able to regurgitate it on demand? The expectations are unrealistic and the reality is incongruous of what society expects of a police officer.

We haven't figured out yet that the brain is far mightier than any weapon we can create physically. How do we teach that? We employ educated police officers with skills beyond those they have from High School. And you have to start by planting the seeds in the community; people have to understand that policing cannot be separate and apart.

Policing must evolve, it must move to the next stage. It's being held back by Neanderthal attitudes about what policing is, we've relegated it to only Law Enforcement. The typical cynical cop thinks kicking butt and taking names is what he's supposed to do; he's misguided, misdirected. If he has no understanding of what the real job is I suggest he moves on; it's time to bring in a new breed of police officer.

We have to re-educate the public first. Why? Because they have come to accept that brawn is better than brain. The classic example is the Rodney King incident that took place in LA. What was so amazing about this case is not that he got his butt whipped and that someone caught it on video, but that twelve people sat on a jury, watched the video tape, listened to the historical account of the police officers lying, and said, 'I don't see anything wrong with that', and acquitted the officers.

Cops take care of cops. The cops beat up Rodney King and other cops lied for them. It's damn near impossible to fire a cop in the United States, they can do almost anything. Here's a true story: a police officer gets found in a Motel room, while he's on duty, snorting cocaine. I should be able to fire him on the spot but it takes over a year and a half. The Police Union says, 'Maybe he's got a drug problem', but I don't give a damn. If he's got a drug problem he shouldn't be a cop. He shouldn't be snorting cocaine and carrying a gun.

Opposite:
A group of Bosnian children in a village near Brcko.

IPTF monitors from Jordan and India observe a situation in the Brod suburb of Brcko.

What we've done is hand over all responsibility of policing the police to the police. The community needs to take that back. As citizens we need to take some responsibility for what our police do. That means I establish a Citizens Review Panel and one of the criteria should be that you can't be on it if you are a current or a former police officer, with the exception of one current officer who would be there as an advisor. Let's take the reasonable citizen's perspective, that's the one we should be using in policing, not the jaded one of us versus them in which the only good people are other cops.

Brcko is like any other part of the world: it needs good policing. The foundation of any solid civilisation is in its ability to police itself, it's ability to self regulate; if you can't self regulate you're destined for anarchy. Why Don Grady in Brcko? Because Don Grady believes that wherever they need good policing he should be there to help them get it. So I bring these ideas of how we do real democratic policing which allows the citizens tremendous input into the policing process.

But the Bosnian Serb Republic police don't feel they need anyone to come in and tell them how to do policing. The international community disagrees and thinks they do need reorganising and restructuring, they do need retraining and they do need to understand something about the democratic principles of policing. So, how do you get an intransigent group of people to become malleable and listen to what you say and do what's necessary.

You can always use the stick. SFOR is here to make sure there's going to be some compliance, but there's always this big stick over your head so if you don't comply we're going to impose some sanctions against you. The best way is to tap into the community and get them to understand what freedom is all about.

If you expose people to enough good they will eventually reject the bad. The best teacher is example. If you see good policing being done you want to emulate good policing; it becomes a reality; people see it, they feel the effects and they crave it, they want more of it.

The police officers in Bosnia are people that are not well revered for their intellectual prowess. They're taking guys that don't make it in High School and sending them to a police High School. If you're doing poorly intellectualy at High School they say, 'Okay, you can be a cop.' But I disagree with that whole theory of policemen being just hired thugs to take care of our crime issues.

They need to be intellectuals, police officers need a higher level of learning. A High School education is not enough in the Free World and it's not enough here. We have to go beyond; we have to have people with the capacity to do policing in a much bigger, broader way, we need people who can think and create new solutions. Policing can't be done as it was in the eighteen hundreds; it has to change, to grow, to evolve and the way that happens is to make sure the people in charge of police organisations are intellectuals capable of being visionaries.

Unfortunately the government here is very centralised and the problem we're having is that those who want to change things are trapped in the middle and they cannot disobey the orders of those at the top. There are some citizens here who may not like what's going on but they're forced to be involved because you do what you're told in this kind of environment. I find we don't get the kind of co-operation they talk about, not because they don't want to but because they can't defy the top.

IPTF and SFOR monitors witness an argument between Bosnian police (in green) and Bosnian Serb police (in blue) about the exact location of the orange coloured IEBL (Inter Entity Boundary Line) marker. Mahala village is one of the few formerly Muslim villages, now under Serb control, that has been re-occupied by Muslims.

*A group of elderly Bosnian refugees
waiting by the side of the road,
near Brcko.*

The basic working class people here are very hard working, I see people getting up at sunrise and they don't go to bed until long after the sun has gone down. I think there's a real desire for peace here, a real longing, even a pain to have peace; to be able to settle and talk to old friends again and see people they used to live next door to. But the government isn't ready for that; the push is to have everything separate, apart, and the people are really struggling with themselves because they're not allowed to go and be friends again.

Bosnia Herzegovina is not like America so I find myself changing, adapting to the local environment; and then I find myself at odds with what Americans do. I recognise that we're incredibly selfish, we're lazy and we're not as good as I would like to think we are. Life has been too good to us for too long; there is no hardship for the most part. If you ask an American to do thirty minutes overtime he gets paid time and a half and will complain. Here they work fourteen hours a day. You begin to rethink what your values are; how much you've come to expect when really we don't have the right to expect at all.

There were some assumptions about how we're going to get the refugees and displaced people to return to the Brcko area. We tell them it's okay to return and they come home. Somebody forgot to say that there is a group of people out there who are willing to kill to ensure they don't come back. That changes everything and protecting those returnees becomes an IPTF problem, particularly when you realise that the very group that should protect these people are part of the group who says they will kill before letting them back.

One of the many thousand destroyed and booby trapped houses in Bosnia; these ones are in Brod, Brcko.

We're trying to manipulate and struggle to make it all happen but it's difficult when we have no executive authority, no weapons and we have to rely on the Bosnian Serb Republic police for protection. We've got a problem. It's like saying, 'As a black man, do you find your life more complicated now that you are working inside the Ku Klux Klan?'

I think the people who move back are terribly brave, or terribly foolish. I don't know if I would have the kind of fortitude it would take to move into an area where people want to kill me. I think I'd be inclined to say life is too short for me to spend it looking over my shoulder looking to see if someone's going to take me out. I think I'd go someplace else.

Had I been a slave what would I have been willing to do to get my freedom? I probably would have been willing to die. I understand why people want to move back, I also understand that it takes a lot of nerve, a lot of strength and I admire those people. Without the SFOR presence my job wouldn't exist. We're sitting on a powder keg. This peace is a very very tenuous one; take SFOR away and the place explodes, they need to be here right now in the numbers they are in. Take them away and you take away any potential for making things change for the better. We would be unable to continue without them.

If all the international community wanted was for the world to believe we have done our part, we showed up, then you can leave within a year; the world would say they came, they tried but it didn't work. If they actually walk out of here in one year this place will not remain stable; it can't remain stable, the hatred is too deep, there's an unwillingness amongst the leaders of this country to work together on anything. There will be no compromises. The international community is going to have to recognise that its presence here cannot be short term, unless they're willing to accept the genocide of one group or another.

Brcko really is a key. The Serbs clearly believe that this is an area that must be held by them in order to link the two parts of what they want as an independent country; they don't want to be a part of Bosnia Herzegovina. If Brcko really is the choke point they are not going to give it up.

The Bosniacs (Bosnian Muslims) feel as though Brcko has been ethnically cleansed: it was eighty percent Bosniac before the war and it's now ninety nine point nine percent Serbian. It was in fact ethnically cleansed. If Brcko is awarded to the Serbs what the international community will have done is legitimise genocide and ethnic cleansing, and they can't afford to do that.

It appears to me that the only reasonable solution is to maintain it under UN rule, an international government, and that multi-ethnicity is someting that is done by decree and not just allowed to take place according to the goodwill of the people now living here. We're going to have to open the city up and do things by decree; but is that really fair? I don't know if it's fair but life, is it always fair?

What do you do after Brcko? I went home for a short while and found watching TV trite; I find the problems Americans want to talk about trite by comparison. What do you do as a Chief of Police when you've been dealing with issues surrounding genocide, ethnic cleansing, serious Human Rights violations, refugees and displaced people returning home? What is it in the American policing system that won't seem mundane?"

*French Foreign Legionnaire
on exercise in Mostar.*

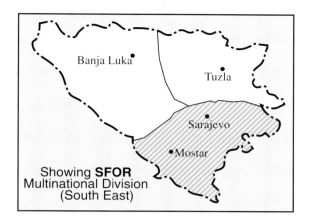

Showing **SFOR** Multinational Division (South East)

Sarajevo, Mostar and Herzegovina

The French led SFOR division is headquartered in the southern Bosnian city of Mostar and its operational area includes Sarajevo, the capital of Bosnia Herzegovina, as well as the mountainous plateau of south east Herzegovina. In the American and British sectors the landscape is more forgiving, the hills lower and more gentle than the bleached, rocky peaks and barren plateaus of Herzegovina. One of the most dramatic routes in Bosnia is the road from Sarajevo to Mostar. It is a miracle of modern civil engineering that follows the line forged by the mighty, astonishingly turquoise-blue Neretva River. The road, carved through rocks and mountains, is a symbol of man's domination over the forces of nature.

Situated in a steep valley divided by the Neretva, Mostar is perhaps the most beautiful city in Bosnia. During the Yugoslav era Mostar was a major tourist destination and visitors from all over the world came to see the ancient Turkish bridge, now destroyed, rising high above the fast flowing river. Now the river is a symbol of the bitter division between the Croat and Muslim held sectors of the city, a powder keg within the Federation. The war in Mostar was particularly vicious. In the early stages it was the subject of a Serbian offensive to take Herzegovina and for six days the city was shelled mercilessly from the hills above. The local Croats were the first to form defence brigades and together with hastily formed Muslim units managed to stop the Serb advance. However, this solidarity soon collapsed under Croatian pressure to set up a Croatian mini-state within Bosnia and by 1993 the Croats and Muslims were fighting each other.

Mostar is a small city and the front line between the Muslims and Croats cut through the centre of town and the war took the form of punishing house to house street fighting. The Croat side was heavily reinforced with weaponry from the Croatian Army but they lacked the will to flush out the now-desperate Muslim infantry who managed to hold their line despite a continual barrage of mortar and sniper fire. The

Opposite:
Aerial view of typical Herzegovinan farmland, near Mostar.

A Ukranian member of the French-German Brigade guards a Bailey-bridge on the Neretva river valley route to Mostar.

Muslim side of the city was completely cut off and the only supply route was an arduous trek through the chain of mountains that leads north to Sarajevo.

In 1992, a Spanish UN Battalion was made responsible for the Mostar area but fighting was so intense that they were unable to keep the aid routes open and were only able to get into the city itself on a few occasions. Today Mostar has an uneasy atmosphere that is reflective of the hidden tensions that still fester between Muslim and Croat nationalists and, despite the massive investment the European Union has made in unifying the city, these bitter divisions remain. Mostar now comes under the operational responsibility of the Spanish SFOR brigade and it appears that they feel particularly attached to this town. In addition to the Spanish units there are also French, German, Ukranian and Moroccan units on standby. The Spanish brigade is based in the Croat town of Medjugorje and their area of operation stretches down through the Herzegovinan plateau to the south east border with Montenegro. Although only a village, Medjugorje is famous amongst Catholics the world over as a sacred pilgrimage site.

Driving east from Sarajevo brings you to an equally spectacular river valley, the Drina, the river that historically marked the border between Bosnia and Serbia. This too is a huge and powerful river that forces a turbulent passage through high, barren mountains and passes ancient and beautiful towns. One of the last big civil engineering projects carried out by the Yugoslav state in Bosnia was the Drina Valley Highway, another miracle of road-building that includes over twenty tunnels and cuts through rock faces so steep that a mountain goat would have trouble negotiating a route. It was against this backdrop of scenic beauty that the terrible war crimes were carried out in the Drina Valley by Serb paramilitaries in the early months of 1992. Hundreds of thousands of Muslims were driven from their homes and sent westwards on foot. The once Muslim towns of Foca and Visegrad were the scenes of appalling atrocities as Serbians, using the ancient Turkish bridges as execution sites, threw corpses into the Drina River. Other notorious towns in the French divisional area are the former UN safe haven of Srebrenica where most of the male population were massacred, and Pale, the capital of the Bosnian Serb Republic and home to indicted war criminal Radovan Karadzic.

The French Army has a respectable pedigree in Bosnia going back to the outbreak of war in 1992. Sarajevo has always been their domain and during the war whilst operating under the unworkable UN mandate the French were placed in the terrible position of having to witness the seige of this once great European city and being unable to do anything to help the people. The rogue Bosnian Serb army, supplied and funded by Serbia proper, took the citizens by surprise and began shelling the city from dug-in artillery positions on the surrounding hills. The people of Sarajevo were cut off from the rest of the country and remained so for the duration of the war. All able bodied men were drafted into the defence of the city and the force that emerged included some Serbs who did not believe in an ethnically pure Serb fatherland. Food became terribly scarce and the only supplies that made it into the city were flown in by UNHCR (United Nations High Commission for Refugees) transport planes to the French-controlled airport as well as occasional aid agency trucks.

Water supply was another weapon used by the Serb forces and in Sarajevo and many other front-line towns the water was cut off. The snipers who surrounded the

The Pope visits Sarajevo and thousands of Bosnians watch him from the stadium that was built for the 1984 Winter Olympics.

city often targeted civilians who were weighed down with their water containers or queuing at communal taps. The seige effectively cut off the Bosnian government from the rest of the country and the result was that areas like Zenica, Tuzla, Mostar and Bihac developed their own local governments that operated with a high degree of autonomy. When peace finally arrived at the end of 1995 Sarajevo was the first to benefit; the seige was lifted and the Serbs were obliged to pull out of the strategic areas surrounding the city. Now Sarajevo is almost a normally functioning city again with water, electricity, plenty of traffic, and rebuilding projects in every district. However it is now controlled by an all-Muslim government and with the loss of so many of its Serbs, Croats and Jews the city has lost the multi-ethnic make-up that was once its hallmark.

The French Division is the most multi-national of all the SFOR divisions. The official line is that it is the most mixed operational unit to have been deployed since the creation of NATO and this mission's example will pave the way for how future deployments will be run. The divisional headquarters is situated in Mostar airport, and the buildings are staffed with officers from France, Germany, Italy, Spain, the Ukraine and Morocco. Surprisingly, the units function together very smoothly and the language problems one would expect are minimal. This is mainly due to the fact that the NATO chain of command is straightforward, the SFOR mission very clearly defined and their system of management sufficiently open to take into account all the views and needs of the various nationalities that may arise.

French SFOR troops patrolling the former frontline area of Dobrinje, Sarajevo.

The best example of nations working together can be seen in the French-German brigade which is based in a suburb of Sarajevo. This is a new type of NATO unit which is made up of French and German soldiers who work together in the same platoons, share the same bedrooms and communicate fluently in one another's language. The appearance of German soldiers on Bosnian soil was initially considered a risky venture because of the terrible history of the German Wehrmacht in Yugoslavia in the Second World War but, to date, all seems well. Their deployment in Bosnia represents a major step forward for Germany as their post World War Two constitution stated that German troops could not be sent into other countries. The constitution has now changed and their involvement in the SFOR mission is symbolic as Germany is anxious to be seen as an equal within NATO, rather than a potential threat to international security.

A Ukranian battalion and an Albanian company operate under the command of the French-German brigade. The Italian Brigade has the responsibility for the large area to the west of Sarajevo, including the Muslim enclave of Gorazde and the Drina valley. Under their command are units from Portugal and Egypt.

Several officers pointed out that they often use the multi-national make-up of this division as an example, when speaking to local ethnic leaders, to demonstrate how easily different nationalities can work together. However, this viewpoint does not take into account that under the former Yugoslavia the constituent peoples used to be totally integrated in schools, towns, the public services and the armed forces. An exception to this was in the Officer Corps of the JNA (Jugoslav National Army) which was dominated by ethnic Serbs. The people of Bosnia have a very clear memory of working together, and many long for those days again, but circumstances have forced them into separate camps where loyalty to the ethnic cause is all-important. Undoing these divisions, at least for the moment, is proving almost impossible despite the immense efforts of the international community.

German Army repair workshop in the Sarajevo glass factory.

*Portuguese SFOR troops on patrol on
the road to Gorazde, Drina Valley area.*

The French Division Interviews

Yves Le Chatelier
Major General, French Army.
Commander of the SFOR
Multi-National Division, South East.
Interviewed at Mostar Airport.

Portrait of Major General Yves Le Chatelier, Commander of the SFOR South East Division. Division headquarters at Mostar Airport.

"I have one third of Bosnia Herzegovina, an area that contains most of the country's hot spots: the capital Sarajevo; Pale, a kind of capital for the Bosnian Serbs; Mostar which is a very famous and beautiful city; Gorazde, a very symbolic Muslim town which is completely surrounded by Serbs; and Stolac which was an ethnically mixed town but is now one hundred percent Croat. It's a very interesting area.

The SFOR mission's first task is to ensure the former warring factions do not re-start the game, the war, so we control their movements, their activities and their storage facilities. A second part of the SFOR mission is to support the international agencies who are in charge of the biggest part of the job — restoring civilian life. We are behind IPTF in trying to restore law and order, behind UNHCR which is in charge of resettlement and OSCE (Organisation for Security and Co-operation in Europe) which is in charge of elections.

Some days we have good signs and then the next day it goes back again. For example here in Mostar we had a very hard period when people shot at our vehicles, but now we're seeing good co-operation between the local police forces and that has come as a surprise. On the occasion of the Pope's visit we've seen something incredible — buses full of Croatian nuns travelling to Sarajevo to attend the Papal Mass and being helped on their journey, through the night, by the Bosniac (Bosnian Muslim) police.

We were expecting trouble and I had four thousand five hundred of my troops on the trail, day and night. Anything was possible as the Neretva valley is very steep and narrow, it would have been easy to hold an ambush every hundred metres. I was also in charge of the security inside Sarajevo and my division had to make anti-sniper missions and prevent anybody from shooting the Pope. This told me that when these people want they are able to be unified, to have law and order, peace and co-operation.

The Dayton Peace Agreement has been assigned to create the state of Bosnia Herzegovina, a state which is made up of two entities: Republika Srpska and the Muslim Croat Federation. However, the Muslim Croat Federation is a concept that has a meaning in Sarajevo and everywhere else in Bosnia — but not in Mostar where the two partners are facing each other directly. Practically speaking, here in Mostar, the Federation is a nonsense. In Sarajevo it works."

Members of the French Foreign Legion sing and march in formation. Mostar.

Hans Otto Budde
Brigadier General, Bundeswehr (German Army).
Commander of French-German Brigade.
Interviewed at Rajlovac SFOR base, near Sarajevo.

Brigadier General Hans Otto Budde, commander of the French-German Brigade, standing in front of a German-built de-mining tank. Rajlovac, Sarajevo.

Opposite:
A partly destroyed stained glass window in a Bosnian church near Sarajevo.

"We have had the Bundeswehr (German Army) since 1956. For a long time after World War Two it was very difficult for the Europeans and Americans to imagine that there would ever be another German Army, but in those days there was a very important threat from the Soviet Union and there was a need to prepare for the defence of Germany and the central region of Europe. Now the Bundeswehr has three hundred and forty thousand soldiers and it's able to increase hugely through the reserves. Every year a hundred and twenty thousand people go through the army, training in case of war.

This brigade proves that one can really learn one's lessons. There have been hundreds of wars between France and Germany and we have been enemies through the generations — until 1945. Now, the example of this brigade proves that we can not only co-operate but we can live together in one garrison, our conscripts live in the same rooms and work in the same offices. This helps in Bosnia when dealing with the locals, particularly with the Serbs, as they don't just see the German Army, they see the Germans with a family of other nations.

During the Second World War the Wehrmacht (the Nazi German Army) was everywhere, including Yugoslavia and France. My father took part in a tank attack in France and my grandfather was nearly killed at Verdun in the First World War. My family knows all about wars between France and Germany and so it feels quite remarkable to be in charge of a French-German brigade.

In Germany there are about three hundred and twenty thousand refugees from the former Yugoslavia. I think most Germans are glad we could help a little bit; we haven't forgotten that we got help from all over the world after the Second World War. But, as you can imagine, there are some Germans who say that they have to go back in order to build up their country. These refugees get welfare payments and the last two years alone has cost the German government about eighty billion Deutschmarks.

There are some regions where the refugees can go back. There's no reason why a Croat from the (Croat controlled) Kiseljak area has to stay in Dusseldorf or Munich. But there are other areas like Trnovo, Dobrinje, Stolac and Brcko which are very

sensitive hotspots and people should not be forced to go back to these areas. One has to deal with this problem very carefully because they are all human beings and we don't want to find a solution that has been drawn with a sword.

The Bosnians are very open to my soldiers and very pleasant to me. They often thank me for helping them — many people have relatives in Germany and a great deal of money is sent from people living in Germany to people here. The relationship between Germany and Bosnia is very strong, for example there have been Bosnian restaurants all over Germany since the nineteen fifties."

Qemal Shkurti
Major, Albanian Army. Commander of Albanian Rifle Platoon. Interviewed at Rajlovac SFOR base, near Sarajevo.

Major Qemal Shkurti, commander of the SFOR Albanian Rifle Platoon. Rajlovac, Sarajevo.

"**O**ur people are not Slavic, not Greek, not Latin nor Italian. We're unique and our language has nothing similar to any other language. They say that we, along with the Greeks, are the oldest people in the Balkans. The Albanians are a very friendly and open people. The word for Albania in our language is Shqiperi.

Under Hoxha, the last Communist dictator, our Army was very big and our doctrine was simply to protect the country. We had Russian and Chinese equipment. Hoxha was a very strict Communist, a purist, a Stalinist. But when Stalin died and Kruschev took over, Hoxha denounced the Russians as they had abandoned what he considered the true path of Communism. He then supported Mao Zedong (the Chinese Communist dictator) but when he died the same thing happened. By the nineteen eighties Albania had become completely isolated, we had no friends anywhere in the world.

I was born in that period, in a small town in the south. My father was an accountant in the local factory but the salary was never enough. Just to buy a TV set you needed special authorisation and it was impossible to buy a car. Albania was a very closed country. We could never leave. Our education system was completely atheist and although I am a Muslim we are not strict in our practices. I went to a military school for seven years.

Recently we had a very difficult situation in Albania because of the pyramid investment schemes. People lost a lot of money. I lost four thousand US dollars, but if the system had not collapsed I would have made a profit of one thousand five hundred dollars over a six month period. The people got angry and they took weapons from the army. They were able to do this because the soldiers had lost money too and were unhappy. Also they didn't want to fire on their own people. Now, in the south of Albania, everybody has weapons.

It wasn't easy for the Albanians who were stationed with SFOR when all this was happening because we couldn't speak with our families and find out if they were all right. But the Germans were very supportive and we managed to continue guarding their base. Our mission is to guard the German logistics base, located in the Energowest factory just outside Sarajevo.

There are thirty five Albanians here. It's not so difficult if you are committed and disciplined and this is true in my unit because we are from the Albanian Commando Brigade, but this would not be true in all Albanian Army units. I came here because it's good to have experience. To me everything here is interesting because it is only my second time abroad. My salary is a hundred and ten dollars a month."

A Greek mechanic makes sparks in the Beluga (Belgium, Luxembourg, Greece and Austria) SFOR contingent workshop in Visoko, central Bosnia.

Loic Frouart
Lieutenant Colonel, French Foreign Legion.
Interviewed at Mostar Airport.

Lieutenant Colonel Loic Frouart in the officers bar at SFOR Division South East headquarters at Mostar airport.

"I do not know a lot about the desert as I've never been stationed in Chad or the Sahara, where the Legion are active, but I do think the desert and the jungle are very similar: you always feel isolated, navigation is very hard, you have to continually keep checking your compass, you always have obstacles. It's very easy to get lost.

In the jungle the main problem is finishing the day and realising you've only covered five or six kilometres. The routes on the maps are never accurate enough and due to the terrain the satellite cannot distinguish the human trails, only the main features such as the big rivers. You're always wet and at night it gets very cold. When you sleep in the heart of the jungle you're always cold, tired and wet; in order to survive you need to be in good condition and you need to like this kind of environment, otherwise you'll quickly feel sick and incapable. The jungle is a very enclosed environment and some people feel oppressed and become claustrophobic. You need to know what you can eat, you need to learn to live off the land. Sometimes you see wild animals but a human is very noisy and the animals tend to flee, even the snakes.

I spent two years in an isolated post in a small village called Regina in French Guyana, just north of Brazil. I saw some jaguars once or twice and some ant eaters and tapirs, plenty of snakes of course, but usually what we saw were mosquitos, grasshoppers, spiders — that sort of shit. Ninety percent of French Guyana is jungle, an area of about a hundred thousand square kilometres. I love it there.

The Legionnaires are always at ease in operational situations, whether they are in a desert, a jungle or an urban environment. Training in urban combat is particularly important because if a war is declared now there's a ninety percent probability that the fighting will be in the cities. So, we were not unprepared when we came to Bosnia, the only difference is that here we carry out a lot of humanitarian missions.

"C" Company (Troisieme Compagnie) of the Second French Foreign Legion Infantry Regiment have just finished their fourth tour in Bosnia. Their first missions were under UNPROFOR when they were guarding Sarajevo Airport. That was a very difficult mission. The problem was that the UN had been handed the airport by the Serbs and they set up a neutral zone. As a result no locals were allowed to cross the airport in their continual attempts to escape Sarajevo.

Our position was badly accepted by the Bosnian side because we denied them the possibility to cross, but if we had closed our eyes at six every evening and allowed people to cross the runway the Serbs would have shot them all and we would have had to collect the corpses in the morning. In October 1993 we had eight hundred attempted crossings every night. We would patrol the airport in our APCs (Armoured Personnel

Carriers) with their lights switched off so the Serbian snipers couldn't see our position. Whenever we found people crossing we would stop in front of them, blocking the line of site from the Serb lines.

The UN system had a two key command system — one civilian, one military — and so it was very difficult to get rapid decisions. However, I think it's unfair to criticise those who served in those missions. The French Army has been here since 1993, seeking peace for the Bosnian people whatever their religion. The French people have lost seventy brothers here for a war that wasn't theirs. But it had to be done, the sacrifices, because these women, children and old people have to be allowed to live normally, to be protected from the craziness of their political leaders. What's important is to recognise the sacrifices of those who were killed and wounded here, without whom SFOR and the peace in Bosnia could not have happened.

I think SFOR has a very difficult mission; it has to maintain the IFOR mission, but that was a specific military mission that separated the warring factions. SFOR has to maintain the peaceful climate achieved by IFOR and hand over to the local civilian authorities. This is very very difficult. There's something perverse in this present situation because it is very quiet and some could argue that SFOR is nothing but a military occupation; on the other hand if we leave perhaps the war is ready to start again.

We have to maintain a military presence with fewer and fewer military missions to carry out; at the same time we have to be ready to react, and to react strongly and overwhelmingly if necessary. If there is an incident in Mostar tonight we have to be ready to react the following hour. I think it's going well because all the troops are deeply committed to the principles of the Dayton Peace Agreement, and I really hope the leaders who signed are going to respect the agreement so that the civilians can live in peace."

French Foreign Legion practise storming a hostile building in Mostar.

Above:
Legionnaires practise the capturing of a suspected terrorist or war criminal. Mostar.

Below
The targets are lined up ready to be searched and arrested.

Overleaf:
The ruins of castle Herzeg near Mostar; according to locals this was the first inhabited place in Bosnia Herzegovina.

OSCE
The Democracy Teachers

Overseeing the elections in Bosnia Herzegovina is the biggest job OSCE (Organisation for Security and Co-operation in Europe) has ever undertaken. This previously little known diplomatic organisation has burst onto the international scene with a splash; OSCE experts, translators, lawyers and monitors (many of them recruited from other agencies) are to be found in almost every town and city in Bosnia.

OSCE was founded by the European and North American leaders in 1975. For seventeen years it had functioned in harmless obscurity, holding conferences on disarmament and human rights, essentially as a forum for European diplomats. This all changed when the Berlin wall came down and the collapse of Communism opened up eastern Europe.

Their first foray from the conference room was in 1994 when a team was sent to Chechenya to witness the levelling of Grozny, once an oil-rich city, by heavy Russian artillery. Unfortunately OSCE were unable to influence the course of that war and the fighting dragged on until the maverick Russian, General Lebed, emerged with a peace agreement that is still holding.

OSCE's trajectory hit its apex in 1995 when the great powers were meeting with the Bosnian war leaders at the Wright Patterson Air Force Base at Dayton, Ohio. It was there that the peace we are now enjoying was finally agreed, although in a very imperfect form, and it was there that OSCE was given the job of overseeing the Bosnian elections. This job involves arranging elections in Bosnia's two entities and approving these electoral contests on the assumption that the freedom of expression and the freedom of movement exist. The problem is that these freedoms do not exist and the war criminals are still influencing government policy in the Serb Republic.

Morally, OSCE are presented with a stark choice: should they denounce the current democratic process in Bosnia as unworkable? After all, the ruling nationalist parties are deeply undemocratic, have absolute control over the media and their respective ethnic population. But this option would be unacceptable to the international community as it would question the assumption that Bosnia will become democratic as a natural result of the Dayton Peace Agreement.

Or should OSCE pretend things are democratic and going smoothly, rubber stamp the elections even if fraudulent, keep themselves in a job and hope against hope that Bosnia's power brokers will move towards democracy anyway? Unfortunately this seems to be the path OSCE has taken, and the end result is likely to be a permanent division of Bosnia between the extremists.

The general elections that were supervised by OSCE in 1996 were regarded as fraudulent by most objective observers. The International Crisis Group, a Washington DC based pressure group who monitor the implementation of the Dayton Agreement, were particularly critical:

"The OSCE had neither the experience nor the means to conduct highly complicated elections... There was no effective protection against refugees in neighbouring countries from voting twice by first casting absentee ballots and then voting in person by travelling to the country… more alarmingly, preliminary results published by the OSCE showed a voter turn-out of more than 100%… These elections should not be declared free, fair or democratic either. If they are the international community will have seriously undermined its own credibility."

ICG report on elections in Bosnia Herzegovina (22.9.96)

W.G. "Gerry" Robinson, QC
Senior Legal Advisor to the OSCE mission in Bosnia Herzegovina, a former director of the Canadian Liberal Party. Interviewed at OSCE headquarters, Sarajevo.

"I come from Canada, a country of considerable freedom and prosperity. I understood what happened in this country, as have many people, through words and pictures and occasional stories. I was stunned and overwhelmed by the pervasive and vicious destruction of virtually everything I could see when I first arrived. It was infinitely more than I expected even though we have all seen disgustingly graphic pictures of what had happened during the war.

I was more or less prepared to see destruction in Sarajevo and the other big cities but I was not prepared to see kilometre after kilometre after kilometre of devastated and inaccessible farmland which was still sown with mines. Not only were there no people but there were no animals, and you couldn't go into the field or into the farmhouse because you didn't know if the farmhouse was booby trapped and you were almost sure the fields were mined.

I have watched a people of great history, of substantial education, fall into a horrifying situation where all control was lost in the passions that were inflamed. I have watched a decent, cultured, educated people claw their way back from an almost impossible situation to where they are on the brink of discovering a peaceful, happy, civilised existence. This has been a quite extraordinary and irreplaceable experience for me.

In 1996 the Canadian Ministry of Foreign Affairs asked me if I would like to get involved in the elections in Bosnia Herzegovina, and I have been made Senior Legal Advisor to the mission. I am also a member of the Provisional Electoral Commission,

W.G. "Gerry" Robinson outside the OSCE headquarters in Sarajevo.

Children looking through the window into the canteen of the Romanian Engineering Battalion, note the vast steel plant in the background. Zenica.

the body responsible for supervising the preparation and conduct of the elections, creating the legal and regulatory framework under which elections are held.

We went through five levels of elections in 1996, from the collective presidency down to Canton [regional] level in the Federation and Republika Srbska. We had not been able to hold the local elections that had been contemplated by the peace agreements; they had to be postponed to the 13th and 14th of September 1997. The 1996 elections were very difficult and we now understand where many of the weaknesses were — and we have largely filled those gaps.

I expect the local elections to be very effective and to receive widespread endorsement from the international community. That is fundamentally important because the elections are only one step in a large process of building peace and stability in this country and in this region. If the elections go well the international community will remain fully engaged, if the elections were somehow not to go terribly well the international community will hesitate in its commitment to the reconstruction of this country.

In a situation like this the international community's interest is in rebuilding a civil society under the rule of law; that's what the total effort is all about. To stop the fighting the military came in and did an amazing job in providing security and stability so that people can rebuild a decent kind of living. Part of that is elections, introducing a democratic tradition that people can rely on to take control of their own agenda.

Issues are the thing that drive political contests. The issues that have driven this conflict have been largely ethnically based; some nationalist issues crept into those issues. But as the democracy evolves so will the issues evolve, becoming less and less the issues of ethnicity and more and more the issues of prosperity and reconstruction, of the return of refugees. I am optimistic that the issues that will be contested by the various political parties will depend less on the political parties' ethnic character and more on their adherence to an ideology that will lead to peace and prosperity — rather than ethnic supremacy.

I came here as an optimist and nothing I have seen here has made me less of an optimist. The peace agreements are a very complex set of inter-related understandings and agreements designed to create and sustain a single country composed of two political entities and three peoples. I am confident that it is in the interest of the people of Bosnia Herzegovina to ensure that they have prosperity and security; those are concepts that know no ethnic boundaries.

There are plans for the withdrawal of the military in its present form. I understand what they're saying, the nature of their plans, but I also understand that the international community has made a massive investment in terms of peace and stability in Bosnia and southern Europe generally. If the international community's interests were to be put at serious risk by the withdrawal of the military, then I am quite convinced that the military will not be withdrawn. It may be called something else, it may be here in a different form, it may be parked outside the country, but I think it very unlikely that the international community will look at the quality of this investment and simply walk away.

We all want to do things that are in our self interest. When I look out of my window and realise that fifty metres down the road Archduke Ferdinand was assassinated and this started the First World War, I cannot imagine why people say the Balkans are not important in relation to western Europe and the peace and security enjoyed there."

Overleaf:
Members of the SFOR Spanish Brigade in a tug-of-war with Bosnian Serbs in Trebinje, southern Hezegovina. The Bosnian Serbs won the contest.

Below:
W.G. "Gerry" Robinson with local politicians and translators at a meeting in Mostar.

A Bosnian Serb peasant passes British members of the Royal Horse Artillery on deployment in western Bosnia.

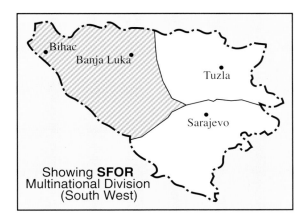

Showing **SFOR** Multinational Division (South West)

Banja Luka and western Bosnia

Western Bosnia is a land of gentle rolling hills, lush countryside and clean rivers weaving through small villages. The gentleness of this landscape is mirrored by the relative calm that this British controlled region enjoys. The British Divisional Area does not contain any major hotspots such as Brcko and Mostar, cities that plague peacekeeping efforts in the other sectors. The cities with the potential for trouble are Prijedor in the Serb held area, Bugojno which is a Muslim majority town with a reputation for extremism, and the Croat controlled town of Gornji Vakuf. However, under this calm surface are the kind of deep feelings of resentment and betrayal that could contribute towards a warlike situation if circumstances were different.

The British Divisional Area consists of Bosnian territory held by the Serbs, Croats and Muslims. All these areas co-exist in an uneasy harmony that reflects the local leaders' acceptance of the status quo but scarcely conceals the fact that this whole country is a patchwork of competing, and largely unsatisfied, territorial claims and ambitions.

As with most of the Balkans, understanding the area requires a glimpse at the history of the region. During the Turkish Ottoman Empire the whole of the Balkan peninsula, including Serbia and Bosnia, was occupied by this powerful Islamic empire. Serbia became an integrated province and Bosnia Herzegovina was developed as a semi-autonomous state that was of vital strategic importance due to its location as a buffer zone on the western periphery of the empire. Beyond the western frontier of Ottoman Bosnia lay Croatia which came under the control of the Austro-Hungarians, a large Christian empire which saw itself as the European barrier against Islam. The border between Bosnia and Croatia became a faultline between these two empires, one Christian and one Islamic, and the security of these borders was entrusted to Serbians whose reputation as warriors was excellent.

Below:
A British Chinook helicopter lifts a 105mm L118 "light gun" and its towing vehicle out of the Banja Luka divisional headquarters.

Opposite:
A Chinook carrying a 105mm L118 light gun, vehicle and seven man crew to a deployment position in Mrkonic Grad, western Bosnia.

These borderlands became known as the Krajina and semi-nomadic Serbian tribes moved into these western areas of Bosnia where they were encouraged to continue their horse breeding and to defend the Ottoman border. In return they were allowed to practise freely their Orthodox Christian faith. Both of these huge empires had been in decay for generations and by the end of the First World War both the Ottoman and Austro-Hungarian empires collapsed and the areas under their control were broken up into the independent nations of Central and Eastern Europe, one of which became Yugoslavia.

By 1992 Yugoslavia had broken up into the five separate states of Slovenia, Croatia, Bosnia Herzegovina, Macedonia and the Federal Republic of Yugoslavia (Serbia and Montenegro). The Serbs had always been the most numerous of the Yugoslav peoples and for much of this century Serbia had been the dominant partner within the Yugoslav federation. Because the Serbs had such large minorities in both Croatia and Bosnia they could never really accept the fact that these countries could become independent nation states outwith their control, and plans to create a greater Serbia which would include large parts of Bosnia and Croatia were developed.

The control of the Krajina borderland areas in Croatia and western Bosnia, where large Serb minorities had lived peacefully alongside Muslims and Croats for generations, became a major strategic objective for the Serbs. These Serb minorities were inundated with vitriolic propaganda proclaiming the immediate threat of Croatian Ustache Fascism and extreme Muslim fundamentalism, and they were then supplied with large quantities of arms. When Croatia and Bosnia Herzegovina declared their independence in 1992 the Serbs in the Krajina regions of Croatia and Bosnia declared themselves as an independent Serb Republic. The newly established Croatian and Bosnian governments were taken by surprise by these carefully planned events and were unable to prevent the Serb extremists from driving out all non-Serbs from the areas under their control. In addition to these conflicts with the Serbs, vicious fighting

broke out between Muslims and Croats in the central Bosnian towns of Gornji Vakuf and Bugojno, and the tensions that first developed in 1993 are still present today.

By 1995 the tide turned on the Serbs. The Croats had built up a large army that was particularly well endowed with artillery, while the Bosnians had hundreds of thousands of battle-hardened foot soldiers, many of whom were refugees. In mid-1995 NATO conducted air strikes against the Serbs and their key communication facilities in Bosnia were devastated. Soon after the Croats and Bosnians launched "Operation Storm', and in a matter of days the Serbian forces had been driven from most of Croatia as well as much of south west Bosnia. So successful was Operation Storm that the Serb-held city of Banja Luka would certainly have been taken had intense American pressure on the Croats and Bosnians not forced them to stop.

On the Croat and Bosnian side the operation was considered a major success. For the Serbs it was a military and humanitarian disaster. Hundreds of thousands of Serb civilians, many of whom had lived in the Krajina borderlands for generations, were sent fleeing eastwards and now these people live as poverty stricken and embittered refugees within the remaining areas of the Bosnian Serb Republic as well as in Serbia proper. The current situation in western Bosnia is essentially unresolved; large Serb, Muslim and Croat populations remain displaced from their homes and none of the three sides are willing to take back those people who are not from their particular ethnic group.

Although a relatively small force, the British Army is one of the most experienced in the NATO coalition. Unlike the German, Turkish and Scandanavian armies which rely on conscription to make up their large numbers, the British Army has been a professional force since the 1950s. Almost every soldier has had operational experience in Northern Ireland and many have served in the Falkland or Gulf wars. The British Army is appreciated for its infantry and the experience of its Special Forces but without the massive logistical and airpower capability of the United States Army they would be unable to conduct large military missions such as the Desert Storm operation against Iraq.

The British SFOR Divisional Headquarters in Bosnia is in the Banja Luka metal factory. It is a tight-knit operation with fewer officers than in the other divisional commands. Despite their large area of responsibility the British force consists of only three battalions and much of the division is controlled by units from Canada, Malaysia, the Czech Republic and Holland. Their approach is relaxed and this enables the troops to go into the community and do humanitarian projects. In 1996 and 1997 a remarkable relationship developed between the British forces and the ODA (Overseas Development Administration) which is the British government's official aid agency. Small building grants were made available to local contractors and these were used to repair destroyed schools, clinics and community centres. The British troops overseeing these projects helped with transport and labour, and completed them at a very low cost. Over three hundred of these grass roots community projects were completed in this way. The other armies under the British divisional command are encouraged to get as involved as possible with their local communities.

Banja Luka is the second largest city in Bosnia Herzegovina and with its tree-lined boulevards and handsome public buildings some say it is the most attractive city in Bosnia. Banja Luka had one of the oldest mosques in the Balkans but it was blown up, along with another fourteen mosques, during the war by order of the city authorities. The jobs were undertaken by professional squads of explosive experts who would appear at a mosque with a truckload of explosives, demolish the building and by the next day the rubble would have been cleared and the site turned into a car park. Many

Serbs from Banja Luka were deeply distressed by this needless destruction but their opinions were drowned by the dominant and intolerant voice of extremism.

So determined are the Serb nationalists to wipe out any trace of their Islamic heritage that they were prepared to destroy public buildings that were considered architectural treasures, and not just by the Islamic world. But what they have really done is to destroy an important part of their own culture. Politically Banja Luka is important because the Bosnian Serb *parliament* holds its sessions there and, as the largest city in the Serbian entity of Bosnia Herzegovina, it should be the capital. But, ridiculous as it may seem, Banja Luka and the rest of the Bosnian Serb Republic have to take orders from the official capital where the Bosnian Serb *government*, as well as Radovan Karadzic, are based.

The Czech SFOR contingent control the area around Prijedor, a notorious town where ethnic cleansing was particularly brutal and an area where several Serb Concentration Camps were sited. The Czech troops were fired on at one point in Prijedor by local extremists who deeply resent the presence of the NATO-led force. The fact that the Czechs are not in NATO and are a Slavic people, like the Serbs, does not prevent the Serbs from believing that they are the victims of a massive international conspiracy against them. Tensions increased in July 1997 when British Special Forces arrested an indicted war criminal in Prijedor and shot dead another who resisted arrest.

The Canadian Army control Bihac and the Muslim enclave in the north west of Bosnia. Their area of responsibility includes an inter-entity boundary line between a large Muslim population on the west side, many of whom were expelled from what are now Serb held areas around Prijedor and Banja Luka, and a Serb population on the east side, many of whom have been displaced also. Fortunately the Canadians have a lot of peacekeeping experience; they have been operational in the Bihac area since the

Malaysian SFOR soldiers, off duty, playing kick-volleyball at Livno in south west Bosnia.

UN days and have succeeded in keeping it under control. Bihac is an enclave that is separated from the main body of Muslim-controlled central Bosnia by large tracts of land controlled by Serbs and Croats and although the roads are officially open through the Croat held territory the tensions are never far from the surface.

Malaysia is the only Asian country that has supplied troops for the SFOR mission. The soldiers themselves consider that coming to Bosnia is a "golden opportunity" to see Europe. The Malaysian contingent control the large southern sector of the division, including a chunk of Croatian-controlled land, a curiosity considering the fact that Malaysians are largely Muslim and the people in their area of responsibility are Catholic and Orthodox Christians. Perhaps due to the open nature of the Malaysians, and their commitment to local community projects, relations with the local population have been excellent. Not far from the Malaysian base at Livno is the Glamoc firing range where SFOR have been given permission to practise live firing with their artillery and helicopter gunships; an opportunity to test their guns in a larger area than is available to NATO forces anywhere in western Europe.

The Dutch SFOR contingent have responsibility for the eastern part of the divisional area and their patrols take them into central Bosnian towns such as Travnik where considerable tensions still exists between Muslims and Croats. Like the Canadians and the British, the Dutch have a lot of peacekeeping experience and have contributed much to this area that might otherwise have remained in a constant state of strife.

Pigs that have grown up under a British Army-ODA funded aid programme are transported to market. Near Banja Luka.

The British Army Interviews

Evelyn Webb-Carter
Major General, British Army,
Commander of SFOR Division
South West. Interviewed in
Banja Luka.

"**M**y father, my grandfather and my great grandfather were all soldiers so there was never really any doubt that I would join the army. I was brought up in very military, some might say unimaginative, surroundings. In 1964 I joined as a private and by 1966 I was commissioned as an officer.

The British soldiers have a wonderful knack of being able to approach locals in a very natural way, without posturing with weapons. Here in Bosnia where peace has been established and we're not being shot at the soldiers can drop their profile, but not their guard, and behave naturally with the local population and try and make the point that we're here to help and not as an army of occupation. If anyone were to shoot at us I would be astonished; and if that were to happen we would change our posture quite dramatically.

Northern Ireland had a tremendous effect on our army. I became an officer in 1966 and we were nothing like as professional as we are now. When we first went in we treated it as if we were dealing with riots in Aden. It was astonishing how naive we were. We were initially welcomed as heroes by the Republicans and it wasn't until later that the current trends prevailed.

For the junior commander, Northern Ireland was the most fantastic training ground, and it's sad to say that it still is. For a young NCO (Non Commissioned Officer) to be in charge of four or eight men on the streets of Northern Ireland, or in the country, was a tremendous way to create a well trained, experienced, confident leader at the lowest possible level. Our NCOs are admired immensely by other nations.

Bosnia Herzegovina is a fault line between east and west and has been for many hundreds of years. A number of empires have swept across this particular piece of Europe and in the process things go rather awry, as they have done here in the last five years. It's going to take some time to calm down.

The Dayton Peace Agreement has been the most fantastic success as it has brought peace, but the civilian side is lagging and is not quite following on schedule. We try and support the peace programme in whatever way we can and every regiment has

Major General Evelyn Webb-Carter, commander of SFOR Division South West, in his office at the Banja Luka metal factory.

officers and NCOs with lots of ideas and energy about how they can help the country. We have done over six hundred humanitarian projects — rebuilding schools and local health clinics with the ODA (Overseas Development Administration) and now we're trying to set up schemes that create employment.

We have arranged for cows to be given to a certain community where a co-operative dairy is to be set up and milk and cheese produced. A young officer came up with this idea and he sat down and produced a business plan; he involved the community, formed a local committee, presented the plan to the ODA and other international agencies and the outcome will be a dairy co-operative in which everyone will be dependent on everyone else. We're doing a similar scheme in the north of the country where we got some pigs together with some sows and helped set up a village co-operative. So far these schemes have been very succesful. The important thing about these projects is that we aim to remove ourselves without leaving an enormous vacuum behind.

These peace support operations are relatively new and it's probably one of the key trends of the future This is probably what we're more likely to be doing rather than crossing the old inner German border and the soldiers themselves thoroughly enjoy it. But our micro-projects are only scratching the surface. What Bosnia really needs to get it back on its feet is massive international investment and massive international aid.

We also try to influence local politicians as much as possible. We initiate dialogues between former enemies and involve the international community in our area; we get people to talk and get them to understand that maybe the military is not as bad as they may have read in their history books. We are here to help and we can facilitate a lot of things.

The different Battle Groups we have are British, Czech, Malay, Canadian and Dutch and it's fascinating to see how each country plays it slightly differently. The Dutch are extremely professional and do their staff work in great detail, they speak immaculate English and so the communication problems are negligible; the Canadians operate in a more British than American way, they've been here for quite a long time now, are very experienced and can provide some very sensible advice.

It's remarkable that the Malays have been involved in this part of the world since 1994; they are very keen but they did find it terribly hard in December when there were temperatures of minus thirty five Celcius at Livno where they are based. But I've been very impressed with what they've done and they've taken a great interest in the community relation projects.

The Czechs are probably the most interesting of them all. It wasn't so long ago that we were looking over the old inner German border thinking, 'who's going to come after the Russians?' They are a very robust battalion, very firm; language is a bit of a problem as not many of them speak English, but in fact this is an advantage as their soldiers can pick up Serbo-Croatian very quickly and they end up having better communications with the locals.

My next job is commanding the Household Division in London District, a remarkable contrast to what I'm doing here in Bosnia. London District is the military district responsible for the capital. Much of what I'll be doing will be ceremonial, involving meeting and greeting members of the Royal Family — about as far removed as you can possibly imagine from being in Banja Luka and dealing with the Bosnian Serb Corps Commander. It's a rather nice contrast between one job as a Major General and another. I'm very lucky to have had the experience of commanding a multi-national Division before going off to a rather more routine type of command."

Beekeeper Dusko Jaric with his bees that were funded by the British Army and ODA. Orahova village near the River Sava.

Ian Pullan
WO2, British Army Catering Corps.
Interviewed in Banja Luka.

Ian Pullan in his office behind the canteen at the Banja Luka metal factory.

Opposite above: A Dutch machine gunner on a Leopard 2 tank patrolling the central Bosnian town of Travnik.

Opposite below: British 105mm L118 light gun and team in camouflaged position in western Bosnia.

"I was born and bred in Leeds, Yorkshire. I believe the northern people are the backbone of the country; that's where all the work was done, that's where the coal mines, steelworks and cotton mills were. The people are very friendly there, down to earth, direct, honest. Unfortunately it's getting like everywhere else now. Where I live was once a nice council estate but it's turning into a nightmare with druggies and all the rest of it.

From when I was knee high I had always wanted to join the army, but I wasn't very good at school and I was very small so I didn't think I would get in. I went to the Army Careers Office in Wellington Street and the Sergeant looked at me and said, 'Stand on them scales!' I was only seven stone. He said, 'I think you should come back in six months time'.

My mother went mad when she heard this as she had spent years trying to fatten me up. I would eat like a navvy but never put on weight because as soon as I'd eaten I'd be out playing football for eight hours — until my mother would stand on the doorstep screaming. She started feeding me cod liver oil and bottles of stout every night, but as much as she was stuffing down my neck I would keep burning it off by playing football. When I went back there was a different Sergeant and he sent me on a selection course. I signed the dotted line, got my four pounds and joined the King's Division.

It was a nightmare. I was really homesick. I nearly binned it several times. I'm the only lad in my family so I'd always been pampered by my mother and my five sisters. I hated it; they'd throw open the door at five in the morning, screaming 'GET UP!' and we'd all have to march down to breakfast together. To us our Corporal was God, we lived in terror of him. The word please was unknown in the army in those days.

Once I got over the basic training I went to the Prince of Wales' Own Regiment and they would initiate you. I was a very late developer, quite a shy young guy, so whenever I took a bath I would lock the door. They would piss in buckets and throw them over me. They would laugh at me having no hair on my chest.

Once I got jumped by six of our lads. They were jealous of the fact that I was with a good looking girl, now my wife. It was her birthday. She slipped and fell on the ice.

One guy kicked me in the head and chest, another held me while a third had a go at me. I vowed to get them back one by one and, by God, I did. I'm not a fighter but that doesn't mean I can't look after myself. I remember getting one of them in the toilets and hitting him so hard that he flew back ten yards, but that night him and three of his mates got me when I was asleep. This went on for four months, until I left the regiment.

Now, eighteen years down the line, I'm still here and I've got qualifications I would never have dreamed of in Civvie Street: Advanced Food Hygienist, Management; even O Level Maths and English. I could run a restaurant, open a business, be an Environmental Health Officer. I've used the Army for my own gains, which is what you should do. You put your years of life in and you have to get out of it what you can. It's been eighteen years of study and experience for me.

The worst experience of my army career was when my Dad died four years ago. They flew me back from Dusseldorf and he was on his deathbed. I was the last person he saw and all he said when I walked into the room was, 'What the bloody hell are you doing here? Have you come to see them bloody Mary's' (Leeds United). It was as if I was meant to be there at that moment. He couldn't comprehend that he was dying. I'm just sorry that he's not here to see what I have achieved.

I was in Northern Ireland where I spent two years in Londonderry, before, during and after the Ceasefire. I don't think we're very well looked after in Northern Ireland: undermanned, overstretched, back to back routines, in the field for a month living in squalor, on for a week, off for a week, away from our loved ones for longer than we would be if we were up to strength. But the troops must get some satisfaction from it otherwise they wouldn't continue to do it.

I moved from one theatre of operations to another, it happened at the drop of a hat. I was asked if I wanted to go on another six month unaccompanied tour. My wife and I were very upset to be separated again, but pleased as well; pleased to be away from the Province, from being quartered in the back end of the earth, moving from unit to unit.

My feet haven't touched the ground here yet. It's a very demanding role, relentless. They say I'm on a honeymoon period but it will probably last until the end of the mission. We're trying to get everything organised for the people who will replace us — getting new ovens, freezers, more modern equipment — plus the routine of providing three meals a day seven days a week. We're the only unit here that have three deadlines a day, and you can imagine what would happen if we missed one of those deadlines.

I think the worst thing about being here is the accomodation. We sleep four to a container and so you have no space. I more or less live in my office but you have to go to bed sometime and then I have to listen to people snoring, grinding their teeth, farting. I'm a light sleeper so I go to sleep with earplugs in, but even so I can hear grunting and groaning noises. I think the army doesn't like you being alone because you ponder. I can see why they think this as there are a lot of pressures and some of the guys can get suicidal. But I don't like having to live on top of other people.

My time in Bosnia has just flown by. The only time I went out was to go to the vegetable shop in Banja Luka. All I've seen is the inside of the Metal Factory. I feel very sorry for the the former Yugoslavia. I know people who used to come here every year on holiday, people who would still come here every year if they could. I would love to come here for a holiday. I almost came here for a holiday once but we ended up in Tunisia. God forbid if we ever pull out; I heard we're possibly moving out but I hate to think what would happen if we did."

Opposite:
The officers' canteen at British SFOR headquarters at the Banja Luka metal factory.

Overleaf:
Dutch mortar team deployed at the side of the road in western Bosnia, the aim of the exercise being "presence".

UNHCR Interview

The United Nations stand accused of being bureaucratic, ineffective, wasteful, corrupt; the list goes on. The wave of optimism in which the organisation was founded in 1946 has faded into disillusion and the good work they do carry out remains largely unheard of by the general public.

In Bosnia, the UN was unable to solve the crisis. Between 1992 and 1995 they formed a military force with a complex "dual key" (civilian-military) chain of command that made rapid decision making almost impossible. Almost all UNPROFOR (UN Protection Force) could do was protect themselves and help deliver humanitarian aid. The problem with the UN in Bosnia was that ordinary people expected some protection, but the UN Security Council Mandate was simply to observe the conflict and supervise humanitarian aid. As a result many Bosnians felt bitterly betrayed.

Bosnia, and the Bosnian Serbs in particular, humiliated the United Nations. The disaster at Srebrenica in 1995, when the UN Safe Haven was overrun by Serb forces and the male population massacred, was possibly the lowest point in the reputation of this fifty year old organisation.

The UNHCR (United Nations High Commission for Refugees) is a different story. Although part of the UN, they are recognised by insiders as relatively unbureacratic

The hand, guitar and cigarettes of a Bosnian villager, near Tuzla.

and often highly effective. The UNHCR is the dynamic arm of the UN, the team that deals with disasters and their human casualties. Often the first to a famine or war zone, co-ordinating aid efforts and helping refugees, they are to be found in remote parts of the world trying to prevent man made disasters from happening, long before they hit the headlines.

In Bosnia UNHCR have an impressive record, in fact their presence was critical all through the recent war. All over the former Yugoslavia they set up national and local offices with a brief to co-ordinate international aid efforts, providing a much needed umbrella for those agencies which were able to help. At the time they provided one of the best means for the international community to channel funds through into Bosnia. Their method of operation was simple and effective: they would give grants to a network of implementing agencies such as World Vision, Norwegian Refugee Council and Scottish European Aid and these "implementing partners" would, for example, bring in convoys of food, organise shelter and essential housing and instal water supply equipment and make conditions for the refugees tolerable.

Now that the war is over, UNHCR have a new and possibly more frustrating mission: to co-ordinate the return of Bosnia's refugees. There are almost one and a half million Bosnian refugees scattered across the world, but very few of them are coming home. Who can blame them? The country has been devastated by four years of war, divided into ethnic mini-states, is run by ruthless political leaders and has an economy that is in ruins.

But if Germany and Japan managed to rebuild their shattered economies after World War Two why can't Bosnia? The difference is political; in Germany and Japan the fascist leaders were destroyed, a new democratic value system imposed, stability established and economic recovery made possible. In Bosnia none of these things have happened and the extremists remain in power. It is as if in 1945 we helped Germany rebuild with Hitler still in power; militarily defeated and forced to co-operate, but defiant nevertheless and obstructing each initiative for as long as possible.

UNHCR is now faced with the seemingly impossible task of facilitating the return of refugees to their former homes. Impossible because the political leaders, particularly in the Serb-held entity of Bosnia Herzegovina, do not want any inhabitants back who are not of their ethnic group.

While there has been a trickle of returns to the areas controlled by the Muslim-Croat Federation in central Bosnia, there have been virtually none to the areas controlled by the Serbs. The situation in the Croat controlled town of Stolac, near Mostar, is chronic; whenever Muslim householders move back the houses are torched. Stolac was supposed to be a model "Pilot Project". Now Brcko seems to be the town in which UNHCR, and the international community, are investing their hopes for a succesful return programme.

In an attempt to break open the sealed internal border that divides Bosnia, to break the ice and encourage ordinary people to travel, the UNHCR opened inter-entity bus lines: Pale to Sarajevo, Bijeljina to Tuzla, Banja Luka to Zenica, Brcko to Orasje. All have proved successful, in particular the Banja Luka to Zenica line which was banned by furious Serb Republic authorities but it went ahead anyway and has proved so popular that you have to book a seat a week in advance.

The following interview was conducted in Tuzla with a UNHCR development worker who was instrumental in co-ordinating food aid in the Tuzla region during the war. He arrived when the Bosniacs were fighting the Croats, as well as the Serbs. The entire region was under seige and food prices had rocketed.

Overleaf:
This ODA-funded bridge, known as Tito Bridge, in Mostar was the first crossing point between the Neretva river gorge which cuts through the centre of Mostar; Spanish SFOR troops are about to cross over to the west (Croat-held) side of the city.

Hassan Khan
Programme Officer for UNHCR's
Northern Bosnia office.
Interviewed in UNHCR Tuzla sub-office.

Hassan Khan, centre, and
UNHCR translator, left,
meeting with a beneficiary
of a UNHCR-funded
housing project in a
village near Tuzla.

"I was raised in a very political environment in Bangladesh. My father was a politi-cian so I was very involved in the day to day politics of the late sixties. In my opinion politics is the highest form of social service. I realised right from childhood that the only satisfaction I would get from life would be to do something for people. I got my inspiration to work with refugees from that time.

I can recall very well when I was six years old having to flee to India when fighting broke out with Pakistan. That was in 1971. As a little boy I had to walk something like thirty five kilometres along a very muddy road. I also remember a political rally in which I participated by climbing on somebody's shoulders.

The people are the best thing about Bangladesh, the ordinary rural people not the bureaucrats. You see how little a human being needs in terms of money and luxury; we have a saying that all you need is some rice, some salt and if you're lucky some fish. Life is simple and people do not expect much from the state. Unfortunately, due to natural disasters, a lack of suitable government policy and the legacy of British colo-nialism, we have not moved very far. Even so, industry is really booming, particularly textiles and tea, and my dream is that one day Bangladesh will be considered a devel-oped country.

I am a development worker. Before coming to Bosnia I was in Cambodia with the United Nations and before that I worked in Bangladesh with a Danish agency and the Canadian International Development Agency. Now, working with a specialised UN agency, I feel very much for the refugees and displaced people because I too was a refugee.

I arrived in Zagreb in July 1993 but I didn't like the headquarters' environment and was looking for ways of getting out into the field. In October I was sent to Tuzla and told to find a flak jacket and helmet and arrange my own transport. I flew in to Sarajevo; we had to run from the runway to a basement and from there transfer to an APC (Armoured Personnel Carrier). There was a terrible noise of firearms and bullets outside. Inside the APC I was afraid because we had to pass a Serb checkpoint and I have a very Muslim name — Hassan — but they gave me no trouble. In Kiseljak I was met by a UNHCR driver and he asked me why I had decided to come to Tuzla as the situation is dire; can't get food, can't get cigarettes. There were no normal roads in those days, only dirt tracks through forests and mountains. It was like the Camel Trophy.

My first night was spent in Tuzla Hotel, but you can't compare the Tuzla Hotel of today to how it was then; the room was freezing, there was no water, I couldn't eat the breakfast because the bread was six days old and the orange juice undrinkable. As we drove to the office I noticed there was no traffic on the road; diesel was too expensive

Opposite:
View of war-damaged
house above Travnik in
central Bosnia.

and the only vehicles were ours or the NGOs (Non Governmental Organisations) that we funded and shared our fuel with.

I had come to look after the food distribution programme in the Tuzla region. Food was a big issue at the time because Bosnia was completely cut off and a kilogramme of flour cost twenty Deutschmarks. Our area of responsibility covered fourteen municipalities with a total population of six hundred and fifty thousand, all of whom were more or less dependent on UN food aid.

We had a food allocation for very basic food items, wheat flour, sugar, oil and salt, of two thousand three hundred tons a month. But we would only receive an average of one thousand three hundred tons, and this had to be divided among the whole population. This situation changed in 1994 when the (Muslim-Croat) Federation Agreement was signed; the roads opened up and goods started becoming available in the shops again.

I was not here when the first great influx of refugees from Srebrenica and the Drina valley came in 1993, but what I do remember is the huge influx from Srebrenica in July 1995 after the fall of the UN Safe Haven. I will remember those two months all my life. We were notified by our Sarajevo office that the Safe Haven had fallen and in one hour I had to work out how to feed and house the thirty five thousand people who were expected. We had a meeting with the Bosnian Prime Minister, Hasan Muratovic, who at first said, 'there is no influx from Srebrenica,' and then he said, 'whoever helps these people will be blamed for ethnic cleansing so I request UNHCR to stay away.'

I came back thinking, 'What are we going to do?' One of my functions was to co-ordinate the work of the NGOs and I called an urgent meeting, briefed everybody and said, 'Be on standby. We may need your assistance.' We then started preparing some

A war damaged house that has been re-roofed and repaired by a UNHCR funded aid programme. North west Tuzla region.

schools as accommodation for the displaced people. Around eight that night a colleague called from Kladanj, the entry point for Srebrenica people to come into the Federation, said people were being put on Bosnian army buses and were heading north towards Zivinice. He then followed the buses to see where they would go. We had been kept in the dark completely, we had no idea of what was going to happen.

As they approached Zivinice they turned off towards Tuzla airport, a UN base at the time. Then we figured out that the intention of the Bosnian government was to put them in another UN Safe Haven. They were quoted as saying, 'These people are UN people, they are not our people; they have come from one safe haven so logically they should go to another.' After some urgent meetings at their headquarters, the UN forces let them into the airport.

For the next seven nights I didn't sleep for even a minute, and neither did any of the drivers or assistants who were working with us. We divided into three teams and worked round the clock. This went on for three months, until the last person was moved out of the airport. It was a rather horrifying experience, but when I look back now I feel comfortable about how we handled it. But the feeling is still there. Why were these people uprooted?

Tolerance was non-existent in some parts of Bosnia Herzegovina during the war, but it did exist in Tuzla city. This has to do with its political leadership. During the war and even today, the Mayor of Tuzla is very well known as a tolerant person with multi-ethnic views. Tolerance has to come from the politicians but they aren't going to be able to enact their views unless they get support from the people. Fortunately Tuzla city has a lot of literate, university-educated people.

There is an obvious sense of security now with SFOR being here. Without the presence of IFOR this war wouldn't have stopped. Even though shooting had stopped around them and people were very tired of war, it wasn't enough. Every winter, and I've survived three of them, the fighting would stop and so even after Dayton (signed in winter 1995) there was a feeling that IFOR wouldn't come, that things would flare up again.

Now there is the feeling that if there is trouble SFOR is here to deal with it. We can now operate in the Serb Republic and I can take my local staff over there. Initially they were a bit hesitant but now they come at thirty minutes notice without thinking much.

It is difficult to predict what is going to happen in Bosnia. In any other country it would be possible to have some idea by looking at the views of the politicians, but here you cannot really conclude anything by their statements. It is impossible to assess what they mean when they say they are in favour of 'open cities' and that everybody has a right to return when clearly, in many, many areas this is not happening and often is being obstructed by the very people who proposed it in the first place.

A year and a half has passed since Dayton was signed but there hasn't been any progress on 'Minority Returns' to the Serb Republic. It is happening in the (Muslim Croat) Federation, not to a large extent, just a trickle, but in the Serb Republic it's not happening at all — except a few exceptions in the Zone of Separation.

By talking to the people of Bosnia, including the beneficiaries of international aid, it is clear that they are tired. They want to go back to their place of origin, like any human being wants to do. But there is a fear about what is going to happen when the SFOR mandate runs out. There might be another war. Who knows?"

Overseas Development Administration Interview

Ever since 1992 when war broke out in Bosnia and Croatia, aid agencies of different shapes and sizes have come to the region to help. Some of these are massive multi-national organisations with branches all over the world, for example the Red Cross Societies, CARE, Save the Children; others are small groups of citizens from various parts of Europe who set up "direct aid" charities and came with convoys of supplies or set up grass roots community projects. Some are highly effective, others useless, while some only do it for the money.

The aid agencies are a relatively new phenomena, their history is closely related to post-war political crises such as the Berlin Airlift, which led to the birth of America's International Rescue Committee. Britain's Oxfam was involved in helping the refugees who fled Hungary following the Soviet invasion of 1956, and many others grew out of helping refugees in post-colonial Africa.

Over six hundred and fifty aid agencies were registered in Bosnia in 1997 and the areas they cover include healthcare, food aid, transport, education, community work, education, demining, agriculture, human rights, construction and job creation schemes. Simply by being here these agencies pump millions of dollars into the local economy every month by hiring local staff, renting offices and spending money. This has been a major stimulus for Bosnia's retail industry which is recovering fast, and the espresso bar industry in particular which is booming.

Many of these agencies work in and around the cities of Sarajevo, Zenica and Tuzla where the local authorities are co-operative and the needs are great. Very few work in the Serb Republic because this area was closed during the war and many agencies object to dealing with local officials who are, in some cases, indicted for war crimes. This is unfortunate as the Serbs have many thousand refugees, often living in poorer conditions than on the Federation side.

The biggest aid agencies are the governmental ones. These are financed by developed countries with substantial aid budgets. The main ones in Bosnia are USAID (United States Agency for International Development), German GTZ (Gesellschaft fur Technische Zusammenarbeit), and from Britain the ODA (Overseas Development Administration). These three agencies in particular appear to have played a major part in rebuilding parts of Bosnia's infrastructure.

The European Union (EU) set up two aid agencies in response to the Bosnian crisis, but due to internal problems one of them failed completely. During the war the ECTF (European Community Task Force) was set up to co-ordinate emergency engineering work. But the money never materialised and the agency quietly disappeared even before Dayton was signed.

The EU's other aid agency is called ECHO (European Community Humanitarian Office). Although bureaucratic and painfully slow in making funding decisions, ECHO has achieved what it set out to do — give money to active aid agencies.

But aid can all too often be a short term investment in damage repair. Many of the agencies plan to leave Bosnia as soon as the situation has stabilised, although when that will be is anybody's guess. The problem is that thousands of people now depend

Opposite:
A doorway to an old house in the Bihac area of western Bosnia, note the Arabic script.

on these agencies, either directly as "beneficiaries" or employees, or indirectly as suppliers of goods and services. The big question is this: will the Bosnian economy manage to generate enough momentum to keep growing after the international community has moved on?

The following interview was conducted with a local employee of Britain's ODA (Overseas Development Administration). Although a government aid agency, the ODA is far less bureaucratic than most and makes rapid funding decisions. Their reputation for effective aid work in Bosnia is second to none.

With a small staff of engineers, drivers and local staff the ODA were able to do much during the war: import food and essential technical supplies; fix water systems, bakeries, heating plants and power stations.

Now the ODA is involved in one of the biggest infrastructure projects in Bosnia: the repair of power transmission lines across the country. These lines cut through the ethnic boundaries and will create an inter-entity dependency that may contribute to the breaking down of Bosnia's internal division. Electricity is one of the key requirements for the rebuilding of Bosnia's shattered infrastructure. If a village is not connected to the power supply, refugees will be unwilling to return home. Most water supplies are dependent on electric pumps and industry cannot function without it. In fact whole areas of devastation are awaiting connection to the grid before repairs can begin.

Ruvejda Hadzihrustic
Engineering Assistant, ODA
(Overseas Development Administration).
Interviewed in Tuzla.

Ruvejda Hadzihrustic, ODA engineering assistant, in the ODA conference room at the ODA Tuzla office.

"Ever since I was a little girl I have been in love with the English language. First I learned a couple of words from the American movies then, in 1984, we started going to Greece on holidays where English was the means of communication. I made friends with kids from all over Europe and English was our common tongue. My teacher at High School was the one who inspired me; she spoke such beautiful English, without an American accent. The last I heard of her she was living in Cyprus.

At school I studied English and German and did Latin in the first year. I specialised in English language interpreting and was taught that there is a very fine line between interpreting and getting involved in a discussion. An interpreter must never get involved in a discussion and that's very hard in a situation like the one we are in now.

We did many subjects at school including the history of civilisation, biology, geography, economics, philosophy, basic law, physics, maths, chemistry, psychology, logic, military training — mine awareness, guns, self defence — and Marxism. Marxism was the worst because by the 1990s Yugoslavia was taking a new economic direction towards the west and Marxism had become irrelevant. Marxism is a utopia; the idea isn't bad, but it can't be achieved. To take from those who have and to give to those who don't have simply can't be achieved. Marxism is not healthy for the people.

The war in Tuzla began on the 15th of May, 1992. I was in the Fourth Grade and we only had a couple of weeks to graduation; they gave us our diplomas based on our previous marks. By June my father thought it would be a good idea for me to leave the country for a few months, wait for the war to finish and come back in time for the University to begin in September. We all thought the war would be over in a few months.

So, on June the 18th I left Tuzla and took the road through Gradacac, Modrica and Bosanski Brod. Soon after, the Serbs invaded that area and cut the road for good. As I was leaving I could see houses burning by the side of the road but I couldn't pinpoint who was doing it. In Slovenia I got refugee status but very soon I was missing Bosnia. The news was horrifying and I felt I was betraying my family and friends; swimming and getting suntanned while people in Bosnia were being shelled. I decided to return home.

My family have always been very close to each other and somehow we never get on well without each other. We used to go on holiday together and even though they were my parents we would have a good time. I was very happy coming home, I don't think I've been happier in all my life than when I saw the Tuzla Power Station. My Dad worked there for forty years and it's a symbol of Tuzla. I'm really attached to it. When we would go on holiday my father would wave at it and say, 'Bye bye Power Station,' and when we got back he would say 'Hello Power Station'.

The Power Station provided work for many many people. My aunt used to work there as an accountant. It's also a very important source of power for Bosnia Herzegovina, it's the biggest in the country. The residue steam goes through heat exchangers and provides heating for the whole town. It would also export energy to Croatia and Serbia when we were one country. The Power Station is inter-connected with all the coal mines in the area, these were called 'Tito's Mines' in the former system.

During the war the people at the Power Station did everything possible to keep us in electricity. At certain stages we were totally cut off and the Power Station managed to operate as an 'Island'; this had never been done before and they were the first to prove that you can operate on this basis. Now it's working again, feeding the system, supplying factories, water sources, enterprises, households.

Confusion is the first word that comes to mind when I think about war. And fear. One day everything is okay and the next it's all gone down the drain. Every day you notice that one of your friends is not there any more, gone either east or west. I basically sat doing nothing, just being, until, in March 1993, my mother, father and I opened a little shop. That kept us going.

I then started working for ECTF (European Community Task Force) which was supposed to be funded by all the European Community countries. The understanding was that the ODA (Overseas Development Administration) would provide engineers, radios and vehicles and the other countries would supply funds for projects. But it turned out that the ODA were the only ones who were paying anything so they decided to change the name back from ECTF to ODA.

Initially the ODA did small projects. They got belts for a conveyor at the hospital power plant, spares for the X-Ray machines, many small water supply projects, fixing bakeries. They kept the Power Station going by supplying bearings for the transformers, tyres for the dumper trucks at the open-cast mines, fixing conveyor belts, supplying miner's cap lamps and fixing the old steam locomotives that were used to transport the coal.

By 1995 the ODA's budget had increased and we were able to do more projects: the heating system in Banovici and Kladanj, the water in Tuzla's hospital; if a village needed a new water supply we would suppply the kit. In those days we would use the BRITFOR (UN British Force) to help us to move stuff in. ODA was good because we had funding. If Colin Gately (Project Engineer) wrote a proposal, we would get it

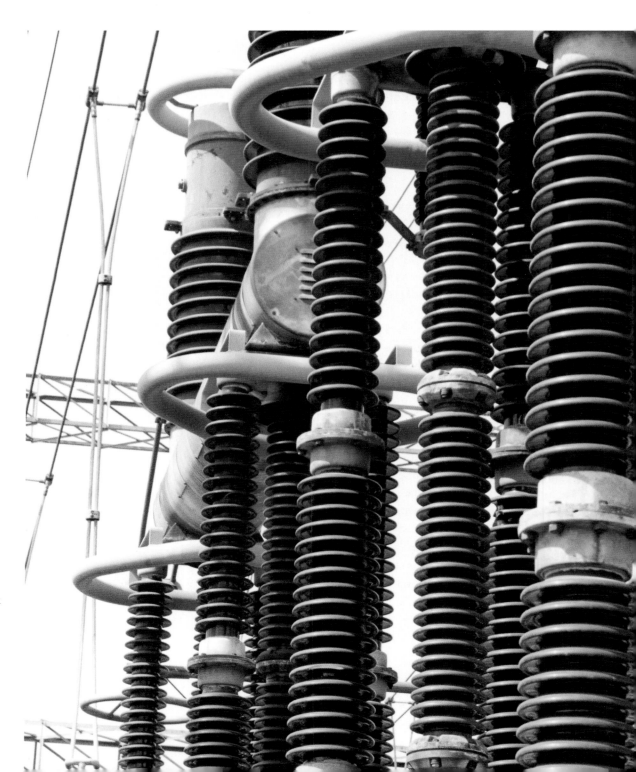

An ODA funded transformer at a power station in western Bosnia (the name and location is witheld at the request of the power station manager).

approved in a couple of days; and then we would know the money was there and we could go to tender and get things moving. We could tell people very soon when to expect delivery. We could act. We didn't do studies and reports and hope that somebody would fund it.

I had a very bad experience with ECHO (European Community Humanitarian Office). I had got used to the ODA's prompt action but on this occasion we had to wait six months for funding approval… and by the time it arrived winter had come. ECHO have done some great stuff, especially when they gave funding, but for us who are used to prompt action it was very difficult

I guess I'm very sentimental about the ODA because it was my first job. I started out as a secretary and now I'm an engineering assistant, which is the highest position for any local staff in ODA. Although humanitarian organisations have done their share, and we wouldn't have survived without them, some send out kids of twenty five to do jobs they have no experience in. The ODA send out mature guys with a lot of experience, guys who wouldn't be caught off guard.

We spent four years waiting for the Americans, Uncle Sam. They were a nuisance when they first arrived. I remember getting stuck behind one of their slow convoys and they wouldn't let us overtake. Everybody here thought they would come into town and spend money but they're not allowed to. They're much stricter than UNPROFOR (UN Protection Force) but this is understandable because they're always a possible target.

Who would dare to shoot at the Americans? Have you seen the arms they have in the Zone of Separation? The United States have the largest number of soldiers here, followed by the Brits and the French. The Americans came with a different attitude. They came to stay, they built special camps with mighty guns we've never seen before. From the way they look they give us a sense of security; they would fight back if they were shot at, not the case with the UN forces.

Bosnia? It's sad, it's difficult, it's improving. Because I'm involved in meetings which gather all sides I can see the improvements. At least they are sitting together and talking. With things like electric power they're forced to connect whether they like it or not.

In other ways I'm disappointed: the continued existence of the (Croat) state of Herceg-Bosna is like a bone in my throat. How can these people claim that bits of land are Herceg-Bosna, when Bosnia Herzegovina is one country with different people living here? Even though Herceg-Bosna is unrecognised by the rest of the world, wherever you go there are little pockets that claim to be Croatian. Everything that happened here reminds me of Hitler and his ideas of a clean race.

Bosnia was such a mixture. My grandmother lived in a street with Orthodox, Catholic and Muslim people and I can't see the reason why it has to be so pure, only one race. There's no explanation why you have people living together in Tuzla, but in Doboj and Banja Luka (in the Serb Republic) Muslims are not allowed home. But Annex 7 of the Dayton Peace Agreement says we are allowed to go home. Why won't they let us back?

I think my country is very beautiful; I haven't seen anywhere so beautiful. It's a pity what we've done to it. I'm not free to walk anywhere because you have these little red signs everywhere saying 'Mines'. The most important thing is to educate the young. We're seeing more and more young people leaving to go to Australia, New Zealand, America. It's sad, but we need to provide the conditions for these people to stay."

Overleaf:
A bridge on the road between Tuzla and Banja Luka is repaired with aid agency funding.

The Minefields of Bosnia

The following report is a summarised version of a document on demining produced by the International Crisis Group (ICG), a Washington DC-based global pressure group. The ICG monitors the implementation of the Dayton Peace Agreement in Bosnia Herzegovina.

The people of Bosnia Herzegovina are faced with a plague of explosive landmines scattered across their country. The other elements of the problem, no easier to deal with, are nationalist politics and international uncertainty about how to respond most effectively to this complicated challenge.

In the former Yugoslavia the basic military doctrine stressed defensive tactics, and the use of land mines was familiar to most Yugoslav soldiers and former soldiers. Thus when the war started in Bosnia, mines were widely employed by all sides.

Much of the time during the war, small, poorly supported units of infantry were struggling to hold tactical positions. Minefields offered a warning of attack, as well as a way to channel enemy assaults into areas that could be covered with defending fire. Moreover, in some cases farmers and other civilians who had become familiar with mines in military training used them to protect crops and property. In other cases, populations abandoning territory seeded houses and urban terrain with mines and "booby traps" to extract a price from the occupiers. This was the case in parts of Sarajevo and many other towns. International demining specialists working in Bosnia comment on the lethal ingenuity displayed by booby-trappers in Bosnia.

The treatment for this plague is a sustainable national demining programme designed with the help of mine-clearing specialists from around the world and the Bosnian leaders. Step by step this programme is coming together.

In 1996, the United Nations created a Mine Action Centre (MAC) in Sarajevo which has been planning the infrastructure necessary to carry out effective mine clearance. The MAC estimates that three hundred square kilometres, of the fifty one thousand square kilometres in Bosnia Herzegovina, pose a definite mine threat, and that another two hundred

A PROM type anti-personnel mine awaits destruction by SFOR troops. This type of mine is triggerred by tripwire and leaps into the air before scattering ball bearings in all directions.

square kilometres are subject to suspicion. These are concentrated along the current Zone of Separation which generally corresponded with the front line during most of the war, but they also include considerable areas scattered inside the entities which were combat zones, and territory which military units occupied or through which they retreated during the war.

The MAC has revised the initial estimates of three and a half million mines in Bosnia down to one million, scattered around nineteen thousand recorded minefields. However, very few of the mines were laid down by military engineers. Most were laid in a disorganised way by infantry or by local defence forces, and were not recorded or marked. This has complicated the demining task in Bosnia and is one of the reasons that UN officials say only a tiny fraction of the land poisoned by hidden explosives, probably less than one per cent, has been cleared for confident use.

The Mine Action Centre estimates that with a national corps of two thousand trained, well-equipped deminers and surveyors — about three times the number available at present — the national programme could clear fifteen square kilometres in its first full year. That figure could increase to sixty to seventy square kilometres per year as the programme makes fuller use of mine-sniffing dogs and as survey teams are equipped with new mine detection technology.

At that rate, the mine threat in Bosnia would be radically reduced in less than five years. But this will happen only if there is an enhanced sense of purpose among Bosnian officials, and continuing support at the international level.

Moreover, the international expertise on mine-clearance is also at a relatively early stage of development. Although the threat to civilians posed by the proliferation of landmines became evident in Southeast Asia thirty years ago, and then in parts of Asia, Africa and Central America, it was not until the late 1980s in Afghanistan that the international community began to develop a coherent methodology for humanitarian demining.

International financial support for a national demining programme in Bosnia has been tentative to date. The United Nations has received only $6.8 million of the $38.9 million requested since October 1996 to support the Mine Action Centre, to develop its data bank, mapping and administrative systems, to establish four regional offices and to build the necessary corps of deminers.

The $6.8 million to support the MAC through 30 June 1997 came from Canada, Denmark, Japan, Sweden, Switzerland, and the European Commission. Other countries such as Norway and the United States have made substantial individual efforts during 1996 and early 1997, and the World Bank has extended $12 million in soft loans to the government of Bosnia and Herzegovina for demining projects in both entities. The Norwegian Foreign Ministry alone has put $8 million into Norwegian People's Aid, a non-Governmental Organisation (NGO) that is considered a standard-setter for the demining effort.

The International Committee of the Red Cross (ICRC), which maintains a detailed data base on mine accidents, reports that about fifty persons were injured per month in 1996 with twenty percent dying, forty percent suffering amputations and forty percent suffering fragmentation wounds. Most are males engaged in field labor, but about twenty percent are children. Displaced persons returning or moving to former front-line areas are frequently victims because they were absent during the war and hence lack the local knowledge that others might have about the placement of minefields.

Mine casualties often suffer grave abdominal, genital and facial injuries, including blindness, as well as the more common crippling injuries and amputations. Since mines are rarely laid in isolation, disturbing situations have occurred with frequency, with relatives or friends injured or killed while trying to rescue other victims.

Many anti-personnel mines are not designed to kill victims but rather to maim them. A badly injured mine victim can have a greater impact on an army, and a community, than a dead one because of the requirement for prolonged medical care, rehabilitation and assistance.

Under normal circumstances, demining is done by individual deminers wearing protective clothing and helmets and moving cautiously through a suspect area, first using hand-held metal detectors to identify metal in the ground, and often lying face down and probing the ground ahead with a rod to see whether the detected object has the size and shape of a mine or is simply a piece of scrap metal. Deminers encounter numerous, time-consuming false alarms, especially in former combat areas where there are shell casings and fragments in the ground. House clearance, which is a variant requiring specialized training, goes even more slowly because of the threat of booby traps with ingenious hair-triggers hidden, for example, in ceilings or under floor-boards.

The process of clearing open land can be speeded up with the use of "brute force" mechanical devices, usually tank-like vehicles that pull or push rollers or "chain flails" across suspect areas to detonate mines in place. Under the right conditions, brute-force techniques can greatly increase the pace, because they skip over the step of identifying individual mines and simply aim to detonate or destroy all mines in their path. They also make mince-meat of the heavy undergrowth that is a hazard for manual deminers in many parts of Bosnia.

But most existing brute-force mine-clearing systems are extremely expensive to buy and operate and are so unwieldy that they can operate only on open ground. At a frustrated moment, one demining co-ordinator dismissed the system his organization has been experimenting with as "fifty two tons of scrap". There is no doubt, however, that some mechanical models can be effective. Humanitarian deminers are particularly interested in testing some new, lightweight, remote-control designs that are cheaper and simpler to maintain, closer in size to an industrial-sized lawnmower than a tank, and hence more manoeuvrable in close quarters.

The process of surveying is critically important because, if it is done efficiently, many suspect areas can be identified rapidly. Sniffer dogs can sharply increase the pace of clearance. But dogs are expensive to train and deploy, tire easily in hot weather, and are only as good as the handlers working with them. Moreover they cannot work effectively in some former battlefield areas because they cannot always distinguish the scent of shell fragments from the scent of mines. There are some new technical innovations under development

An American dog and handler search for exposives in a house near Brcko.

that may accelerate the process of surveying suspect mined areas, but the advanced military powers have been slow to develop them and have not released them for field testing in Bosnia.

Mine-clearing is not necessarily highly dangerous work if it is done cautiously, but it requires great discipline and frequent rest periods because boredom and carelessness can be lethal, either to the deminers or to those who follow after. The ideal in humanitarian demining is to reduce the actual and perceived threat to zero percent. The reality, however, is that a lingering trace of doubt is the inevitable legacy of mine warfare.

Those who engage in demining do so out of a variety of motives. A Bosnian farmer with military experience may accept the risk of clearing his own field because no one else has showed up to do so and he needs to plant crops. Most civilian deminers, however, are unlikely to enter a training programme and demine for a living unless paid a substantial salary.

Commercial companies, of which there are about a dozen with international reputations, come seeking profits. The ideal place for them would of course be Kuwait. Companies operating here usually have to adjust their pay scales and lower their profit margin to what the donor market will bear.

The military forces of the former warring parties in Bosnia inevitably have complicated motives. As long as the possibility of renewed hostilities hangs over Bosnia, it is in their interest to leave minefields that may prove useful in the ground. The SFOR command tacitly recognizes this in its instructions to the faction forces, directing the compulsory mine-lifting activities to "large or high density, easily accessible known military mined areas which were laid by the respective party and to which there is no significant political or military significance or sensitivity."

SFOR officials believe that some of the minefield records that should have been turned over to SFOR have disappeared in a "scorched filing cabinet" policy. They acknowledge that around certain critical areas such as Brcko and Gorazde, which would be immediate strategic objectives if war resumed, Bosnian military units of various former warring parties frequently merely go through the motions of demining.

An additional important contributor is the NATO-led force in Bosnia (IFOR in its first year and SFOR since December 1996). The NATO-led force has done no mine clearance that was not directly necessary for "force protection," that is, for the efficiency of its own operations and the safety of its own personnel. Accordingly, the NATO presence has had less impact on Bosnia's mine problem than would otherwise have been the case. Nonetheless the NATO force has gradually paid increasing attention to the civilian mine threat.

Bosnia's landmine plague remains a huge problem for the country as a whole and to people returning to their homes in former frontline areas in particular. Clearly, the solution to this major challenge is a national demining programme developed by Bosnia's leaders, and international experts, that has the wholehearted support of the international community. New methods of mine-detection, as well as NATO troops on the ground, could contribute significantly to these efforts.

ICG (International Crisis Group), Obala Kulina Bana 29,
Sarajevo, Bosnia Herzegovina. 19th July 1997

The Dayton Peace Agreement
A summary

Following several weeks of intense negotiations at the Wright Patterson Air Base near Dayton, Ohio, the leaders of the former warring parties, under strong pressure from the United States, signed what has become known as the Dayton Peace Agreement. The full title of the agreement is *The General Framework Agreement For Peace in Bosnia and Herzegovina* and it was signed by the Presidents of Yugoslavia (Serbia), Croatia, and Bosnia and Herzegovina. This agreement has become the basis for all peace-building efforts in Bosnia since November 1995.

The main points are as follows:

1. Bosnia and Herzegovina will remain as a single state within its current border. It will be a unified state composed of two autonomous political entities: The Muslim-Croat Federation and Republika Srpska (Bosnian Serb Republic). Under the agreement, both entities will exchange certain territories within a hundred and twenty days.

2. Bosnia and Herzegovina will have a central government, located in Sarajevo, made up of representatives from both entities.

3. The agreement includes a constitution for Bosnia and Herzegovina that creates a presidency, a parliament and a constitutional court. A central bank will be set up with a currency that is common to both entities.

4. The former warring parties will cease all acts of war and will withdraw behind a two kilometre-wide zone of separation (the ceasefire line).

5. The parties pledge to withdraw all heavy weapons and forces to locations identified by the NATO commander in Bosnia. Excess military personnel are to be demobilised and are prohibited from taking part in any further military training.

6. The parties agree to the setting up of a NATO-led Implementation Force with responsibility for the territorial and military aspects of the agreement.

7. The parties agree to the international community setting up an Office of the High Representative to oversee the civilian aspects of the agreement, assist in the setting up of the central government institutions and co-ordinate humanitarian aid.

8. The United Nations will set up an International Police Task Force to monitor, train and advise the law-enforcement agencies of Bosnia and Herzegovina.

9. Free and democratic elections will be held throughout Bosnia and Herzegovina under the supervision of the Organisation for Security and Co-operation in Europe. These will be held at local, entity and national levels. People displaced by war from their homes will have the right to vote in their original place of residence.

10. All the people of Bosnia have the right to move freely throughout the country without harassment or discrimination. Refugees and displaced persons will have the right to return to their homes or obtain compensation.

11. The agreement commits Serbia, Croatia and Bosnia Herzegovina to co-operate fully with the International Criminal Tribunal for the Former Yugoslavia and arrest all known war criminals on their territory.

12. All foreign military forces situated in Bosnia Herzegovina are to be withdrawn from Bosnia Herzegovina immediately.